Praise for *The Hidden Gifts of Helping*

"For over two decades, Stephen Post has produced the most impressive body of work cogently arguing for love's central role at the interface of science, medicine, and spirituality. Most often his books and papers present strong objective arguments, as befits a respected academic, that loving others makes perfect biological, medical, psychological, and social sense. Here in this wonderful new book, he makes the argument 'by acquaintance.' An unsettling separation from a place of attachment and solace becomes an occasion of grace in that he and his family are called to find newly invigorated attachments. They do so with the help of inspiring recollections and encounters with heroes present and past who themselves have found the healing grace of loving others. Dr. Post has given us a heartfelt gift—a modern adventure story steeped in the old wisdom of what it takes to lead a good and healthy life."

> —Gregory L. Fricchione, MD, professor of psychiatry, Harvard Medical School, and director of the Benson-Henry Institute for Mind Body Medicine, Massachusetts General Hospital

"In reflecting on his life's challenges and transitions, Stephen Post weds solid science with practical wisdom and conveys the resulting truths with inspiring life stories. With graceful prose he points the way to human flourishing—through self-giving love."

> —David G. Myers, Hope College, and author, *A Friendly Letter to Skeptics and Atheists: Musings on Why God Is Good and Faith Isn't Evil*

"Stephen Post has long championed the simple but sublime truth that by helping others we help ourselves. He has documented this cardinal principle of positive psychology in a long series of authoritative volumes and research projects, including a major project on happiness that he helped lead over the past five years at Emory.

In this engaging new volume, Post combines touching [auto]biography, philosophical reflection, and scientific findings into a compelling narrative on how and why love of God, neighbor, and self converge. This is a book to be read in an evening and savored for a lifetime."

—John Witte, director and distinguished professor,
Center for Law and Religion, Emory University

"In an elegant and thoughtful reflection on his family's move from their settled life in Ohio to their new home in New York, Stephen Post uncovers 'hidden gifts' among life-changing challenges. As one of America's most knowledgeable philosophers and scholars of the interrelated roles of altruism, love, and compassion in spiritual and physical wellness, Dr. Post brings years of scientific inquiry into critical dialogue with his own family crisis of transition, change, and adaptation. The result is an educational and inspirational chronicle that grounds the foundational belief that helping others does heal and transform human life. *The Hidden Gifts of Helping* offers renewed meaning to the biblical maxim that 'a generous person will prosper; whoever refreshes others will be refreshed' (Proverbs 11:25)."

—The Rev. Dr. Walter J. Smith, S.J., Ph.D.,
president and CEO, HealthCare Chaplaincy

The Hidden GIFTS *of Helping*

HOW THE POWER OF GIVING, COMPASSION, AND HOPE CAN GET US THROUGH HARD TIMES

Stephen G. Post

JOSSEY-BASS
A Wiley Imprint
www.josseybass.com

Published by Jossey-Bass
A Wiley Imprint
989 Market Street, San Francisco, CA 94103-1741—www.josseybass.com

Readers should be aware that Internet Web sites offered as citations and/or sources for
further information may have changed or disappeared between the time this was written
and when it is read.

Limit of Liability/Disclaimer of Warranty: While the publisher and author have used
their best efforts in preparing this book, they make no representations or warranties with
respect to the accuracy or completeness of the contents of this book and specifically
disclaim any implied warranties of merchantability or fitness for a particular purpose.
No warranty may be created or extended by sales representatives or written sales
materials. The advice and strategies contained herein may not be suitable for your
situation. You should consult with a professional where appropriate. Neither the
publisher nor author shall be liable for any loss of profit or any other commercial damages, including but not limited to special, incidental, consequential, or other damages.

Jossey-Bass books and products are available through most bookstores. To contact Jossey-
Bass directly call our Customer Care Department within the U.S. at 800-956-7739,
outside the U.S. at 317-572-3986, or fax 317-572-4002.

Jossey-Bass also publishes its books in a variety of electronic formats. Some content that
appears in print may not be available in electronic books.

Library of Congress Cataloging-in-Publication Data

Post, Stephen Garrard, date.
The hidden gifts of helping : how the power of giving, compassion, and hope can get
us through hard times / Stephen G. Post.
p.   cm.
Includes index.
ISBN 978-0-470-88781-3 (hardback); 978-0-470-94006-8 (ebk);
978-0-470-94005-1 (ebk); 978-1-118-04320-2 (ebk)
1. Helping behavior.   2. Compassion.   I. Title.
BF637.H4P664   2011
205'.677—dc22

2010040024

Printed in the United States of America
FIRST EDITION
HB Printing 10 9 8 7 6 5 4 3 2 1

CONTENTS

INTRODUCTION: ON THE MOVE   vii

1   LEARNING TO TRAVEL ON LIFE'S
    MYSTERIOUS JOURNEY   1
2   THE GIFT OF THE "GIVER'S GLOW"   23
3   THE GIFT OF CONNECTING WITH THE
    NEEDIEST   57
4   THE GIFT OF DEEP HAPPINESS   89
5   THE GIFT OF COMPASSION AND
    UNLIMITED LOVE   117
6   THE GIFT OF HOPE   149

EPILOGUE: ALWAYS COMING HOME   171

Notes   177
Acknowledgments   189
The Author   191
Index   193

To my son, Drew, who had to recreate his life after leaving his native Cleveland at age thirteen; to my wife, Mitsuko, for helping us plant our roots in our new garden; and to my daughter, Emma, who is always giving and glowing.

And to the people of Cleveland, for being as good as they are.

On the Move

L ife can be what we envision it to be, but it is not always what we expect.

In 2008, my old job more or less disappeared out from under me. After twenty years at Case Western Reserve University School of Medicine, my family—myself; my wife, Mitsuko; and our thirteen-year-old son, Andrew—suddenly found ourselves leaving our beloved home in Cleveland, Ohio, to move to northern Long Island, where I had been offered a challenging new job: I would be leading a newly formed team of researchers at New York's Stony Brook University School of Medicine, studying and teaching about the impact of compassionate care and giving on the well-being and health of those who receive and those who bestow. What a wonderful opportunity, but the unexpected enormity of the move—physically, emotionally, even spiritually—was more than we had anticipated.

We were out of place and uprooted. Constancy of place is so important in life if we are to form lasting relationships and deep communities, and if we are to avoid abandoning one another in the name of supposedly greater goods. Now we were struggling with placelessness, and part of being out of place is being out of relationship. This was a serious matter after two decades in a city with all the routines of life that familiarity and constancy of place make possible. Fortunately, we had those twenty good years in Ohio under our wings as we struggled to find ourselves in an unfamiliar place, determined to recreate the good life of community and friendships we all keenly missed. The key turned out to be something we knew quite well, but learned to remember daily in our upheaval: the healing power of helping others. If I am correct, we Americans tend to celebrate our independence from place and community, trying to fool ourselves with the myth that we are more detached than we really are. This myth falls apart in a time of crisis when we really need a community to fall back on. There is much more suffering in our uprootedness than the myth of independence allows us to be honest about. This is a book that looks honestly at our family experience of being on the move, and shows that for happiness and health, rebuilding community through purposeful self-giving and service is absolutely essential.

Rx: help others. This little prescription has the side effect of benefiting the helper, so long as one does not become overwhelmed. Research in the field of health psychology, and all the great spiritual traditions, tells us that one of the best ways to get rid of anger or grief is to actively contribute to the lives of those around us. Science supports this assertion: giving help to others measurably reduces the giver's stress; improves health and well-being in surprising and powerful ways; renews our optimism about what is possible; helps us connect to family, friends, place, and lots of amazing people; allows the deep, profound joy of our humanity to flow through us and out into the world; and improves our sense of self-worth. These are valuable gifts anytime, and particularly when we have lost a valued place and community in hard times. If there is one great secret to a resilient life of growth, well-being, and good health, it is in never giving up on giving.[1]

Eventually, of course, everyone stumbles on hard times. After all, no one gets out of life alive. Today, even those who had considered themselves protected from hardship are being tested and having their lives changed by volatile economic markets, job insecurity, forced moves, and the sudden isolation of placelessness. When we are tested, a deeper kind of learning goes on. This learning is experiential, not intellectual. I like to say that hard lessons are learned hard. In fact, there is no other way to learn life's big lessons than through experience and hard knocks. Even if some wisdom comes from avoiding other people's mistakes as we observe them, most of it comes from all the things that life just naturally throws at us. I have learned a lot about the importance of constancy of place and of the community of relationships that place makes possible.

※

Americans have been a people on the move since the early days of our history. When the insightful French observer Alexis de Tocqueville visited the United States in 1831, he was amazed to see how easily and often Amercians change residences: "In the United States, a man will carefully construct a home in which to spend his old age and sell it before the roof is on. . . . He will settle in one place only to go off elsewhere shortly afterwards with a new set of desires."[2] Being on the move is very American. The "pursuit of happiness" by moving someplace else in search of something better is part of the American ethos. But there is a cost. Researchers have shown that in general, children who frequently move tend to do less well in school and have more behavioral problems; adolescents who move too frequently tend to consume alcohol and have a higher suicide rate; among middle-aged adults, higher numbers of lifetime moves are strongly associated with lower life satisfaction and self-rated global and mental health; in later adult years, residential moves are clearly associated with great risk of death. Introverts have to work a lot harder than extroverts at recreating a social world in a new place because doing so does not come naturally to them, and they suffer more from the loss of connectedness.[3]

Of course there are many for whom moving turns out well. Some children and adolescents flourish in a new place with new friends, and they have a chance to reinvent themselves in positive and resilient ways. Certainly experiences of big moves vary based on age, on the duration and degree of rootedness in the previous community, on the hospitality shown in the new place, and on many other factors that we still need to learn about. But there is no controversy over this reality: in general, loss of community and social capital predicts stress and is associated with elevated mental and physical illness. We need to take Tocqueville's admonition a little more to heart. How we approach moves in life is really very important because the consequences are so significant, and this is why I wanted to write this book. I wanted to help others who are going through similar adjustments.

Americans are on the move in these economic times, and often less because they want to than because they have to! It is so easy to embrace self-pity and get caught up in a spiral of rumination or indifference to others. A first impulse may be to lash out or to hide under the covers until things get better. But when we demonstrate sincere concern for others—whether it's empathizing with a friend's loss, doing grocery shopping for an elderly neighbor, clearing trash from a local park or beach, or volunteering to work one-on-one at a hospice or homeless shelter—we can more quickly improve our well-being and give voice to our deeper identity and dignity as human beings.

The serious study of giving, goodness, and love—the kind of love enshrined in the Golden Rule; the kind championed for centuries by the world's great moral and spiritual traditions, East and West—has been central to my life for many years. As director of the Center for Medical Humanities, Compassionate Care, and Bioethics at New York's Stony Brook University, I study and teach about the ways in which compassionate medical care benefits professionals as well as patients. And in my weekend volunteer role as president of the nonprofit Institute for Research on Unlimited Love, I am interested in the astonishing number of people in America and elsewhere who self-report experiences or intuitions of a higher love in the universe, and who feel that this enlivens and extends their natural benevolence.

In the six short chapters of this book, I share my family's reaffirmation of the healing power of helping others, as well as my passion about how this simple activity—expressed in an infinite number of small or large ways—can help us survive and thrive despite the curveballs life throws at us. We never seek these challenges, but they seem to seek us, and we have to accept them in faith and creativity. Along the way, I'll share other inspiring stories of hardship, helping, and the resurrection of hope and confidence in the essential goodness of humanity. Interwoven with supporting scientific research and spiritual understanding, this book is offered to you as a gift: a true companion and guide to the power of giving, forgiving, and compassion in hard times. I hope you will carry its message close to your heart as the light begins to shine in your life once again, as it eventually will with the passage of time.

Dr. Gregory Fricchione, director of the Benson-Henry Mind Body Institute at Harvard University, tells me that big moves and the anxiety of placelessness involve the slow process of overcoming separation through new attachments to people and objects in our environment. He also tells me that we always underestimate just how much those old attachments and familiarities mean to us. The healing powers of time, of growing familiarity with environment, of self-giving, of spirituality, and, for those so inclined, of a faith community, all can work together as they did for me and my family.

We need to think more carefully about moving on and on again, as though there were no deep costs. Serial movers have fewer "quality" relationships, and children who move a lot in general report somewhat lower levels of happiness as adults. Outgoingness is one great defense against rootlessness, and especially reaching out to help others in a new place. This is what we did, and it worked well. These days, as so many American families have to hit the highways as castaways, we need helper therapy more than ever. The idea of this book is to weave together story, science, spirituality, and practice in a way that will help others who suddenly find that they have to say good-bye to a good place, especially under pressure.

And we Americans need to stop thinking so much about the hidden costs of self-giving and embrace the hidden gifts!

The
HIDDEN
GIFTS *of Helping*

1

Learning to Travel on Life's Mysterious Journey

For most of my early life, all I knew about Cleveland, Ohio, was its nickname: the "mistake by the lake," the place so polluted that in 1969 the city's Cuyahoga River caught fire. In all the years I had driven happily from Chicago or Ann Arbor along Route 80, heading for New York City's George Washington Bridge, I always thought of Cleveland as a strange black dot on the map, stuck up there north of Route 80 on the edge of Lake Erie, a place to be avoided at all costs. But in 1988, the job market called. I was offered a stable salaried position at Case Western Reserve University School of Medicine. So on June 7, 1988, I piled my family's furnishings into a small U-Haul trailer and drove from Tarrytown, New York, where we were quite happy and I had a good job as a college teacher. I headed for the Coventry neighborhood of Cleveland Heights, wondering just what I had done.

My wife, Mitsuko, and our five-year-old daughter, Emma, were visiting relatives in Japan until August, so I spent that supremely hot and humid summer sleeping on a mat on the floor of a sweltering top-floor apartment, the refrigerator door wide open in a failed attempt to cool off. I consoled myself with the knowledge that on a good day, with light traffic, it was only an eight-hour drive to New York City.

But I needn't have agonized: our twenty years in Cleveland were great ones. We soon discovered that Cleveland's unique combination of Midwestern hospitality, great culture, and immense creativity suited us perfectly. And we lived a full life there, in the inner-ring suburb of Shaker Heights. Over two decades, bonds of affection grew naturally in a part of the country where community is genuine. We had no tall fences on our block, just low ones that allowed for lots of conversation between neighbors. Sidewalks and neighborhood schools, lively churches and synagogues, block parties and neighborly warmth made love apparent. When new folks move in around the neighborhood, just about everyone pops by with baked goods and a warm hello. There are lots of neighborly places like Cleveland, where friendly greetings like "Hi Jan," "Howdy Ray," and "What's up, Mike?" point to the connectedness that makes people flourish and stay healthy. Clevelanders defend the quality of their community for a reason. It is an exceptionally giving place, and "love thy neighbor" still means something. For twenty years, we were lucky to call it home. We were a family in place, with all the familiarities, routines, and supportive relationships that follow from being in place. Then, regrettably, our comfortable city—where our son, Andrew, had been born; where my mother, who moved to be near us after Dad passed away, had died; and where I had enjoyed a fruitful career and great local church—was unceremoniously pulled out from under us, like an old rug.

🌿 THE BIG MOVE

A few years earlier, I had gotten a new department head, an ardently secular psychiatrist who I could laugh with but whose ideas for the direction of our ethics program in the medical school ran differently than mine. In fact, we were very different in every way—spiritually, intellectually, ethically, temperamentally. But I loved Cleveland, and my life there. Although I was a tenured professor, my job more or less evaporated. It was like sand passing through a big hour glass until it stops. When my boss told me that I could only stick around if I paid 100 percent of my own salary, it seemed like a good time to call it quits. Being an American, I don't work for free and don't think anyone should. It was pointless to stay where I was not wanted. This sort of thing happens in life, and it happens to a lot of people. It just is what it is. My situation was not unique, and life is not ever quite fair. Anyway, I was offered several new jobs, one of which was at New York's Stony Brook University: visiting professor of preventive medicine and director of the Center for Medical Humanities, Compassionate Care, and Bioethics—with the freedom to stay and hire new faculty. It was a challenge I was looking forward to. There is something to be said for experimentation with a new environment and new colleagues. Stony Brook has always been known for astonishingly accomplished professors, so I would feel like a small fish in a big pond and interact with a lot of great folks in New York City. In these ways, a move can be a really creative adventure.

Despite all my good intentions, however, those first months away were by far the worst that my family had ever experienced. Without question, Stony Brook University is a great place, and I had landed in the perfect position. And the setting is beautiful: the north shore of Long Island is lovely, with rocky beaches and hills much like New England, and with the waves and sunsets of the Long Island Sound. But despite the university's many charming qualities and professional advantages, for almost a year following the move I had days when I felt that my life had gotten off track, that maybe I had dropped the ball somehow. At some level, I still wished that I could have done more for Cleveland. Everyone confirmed that I was doing a splendid job in my new position, but I no longer had the rich social fabric and assumed familiarities of two decades—a gift we so often take for granted until we lose it. I felt some natural anxiety about the whole move because that is how humans who have connected well with a former place and community should feel. My wife and son, like me, were struggling with the adjustment. At work, of course, it was my duty to excel and to view my new situation as an opportunity for learning and growth. That was the easy part.

We had sold our house in Shaker Heights before leaving, but we did not do as well as we might have because the market was slowing a lot. No one could have guessed that it would slow as much as it did a few months later. We jumped into a home near the campus in Setauket, where—like much of New York State—real estate costs are about four times what they are around Ohio. I figured that we had timed the market well and bought at a low, but from August 2008, prices went straight downhill, and nothing had prepared us for the sky-high real estate taxes in New York. Of course one knows about these high costs intellectually, but only with experience does this really sink in. So financial concerns added to our stress, as they do for so many Americans these days. Maybe someday the housing market will come all the way back, but not for a long while. Like many Americans in their fifties who thought they were more or less past any financial worries, I found myself anxious for the first times in years.

Andrew was happy with his life in the Shaker Middle School. He had some good friends, and a first girlfriend. He resented this move deeply, and he let us know through his attitude and behavior. I couldn't blame him. I worried about how the move would affect him, and for the first few months we drove back to Ohio together every four or five weeks so he could visit his friends and take his girlfriend to the movies. This was a good thing because it eased the loss for him and, incidentally, for me. I looked forward to getting off Long Island and out onto Route 80 and the heartlands. I would be singing by the time we hit the Delaware Water Gap where New Jersey ends and Pennsylvania begins. I felt free again. There was good father-and-son chat all the way.

Mitsuko, too, missed Cleveland. At first, she was very excited about moving to New York, where the Japanese shopping is better than it is in Ohio, and where the winters are a little easier. But as soon as we arrived, she began to feel the loss of her friends and her colleagues at the Carol Nursery preschool where she had worked. For better or for worse, I have been the main breadwinner over the years, and Mitsuko has come along as the job market called me—from Chicago to Ann Arbor to Tarrytown to Cleveland to Long Island. As the one stepping into new jobs and work relationships, I have found it a little easier to adjust, at least at first, because I become immersed in my job. Fortunately, the house we bought in Setauket is across the street from the local elementary school, where Mitsuko almost immediately found a paying job helping children with special needs. Studies show how "trailing spouses" frequently volunteer to do community service when they come to a new place. Helping those kids across the street saved Mitsuko in so many ways, and even made me feel somewhat better about buying this now less valuable and overtaxed house.

Our very selves are made up of where we feel most at home. Being in place matters, including all the little intimate details: the river with the perfect waterfall in my favorite Ohio hamlet of Chagrin Falls; a special place to pray early in the morning on the greenest of lawns in front of the Cleveland Museum of Art; a comfortable old chair in the town library; the familiar voices of neighbors and children down the street; a cup of coffee and conversation at the local Arabica coffeehouse with my old friend Tom; Dr. Robbins, our kind and dependable dentist; and Dr. Vizzy, the physician with excellent listening skills that make her patients feel loved. Cleveland wasn't just any place; it was *the* place we were tied to. Now home was somewhere else, but not really, not yet, and maybe not ever.

Our anxiety was rooted in placelessness, a lost sense of connectedness not just with people and a city that had been good to me but with my own soul and vision. Our minds are so grounded in place and relationship. The idea that our minds are above the world and free like birds on the wing is untrue.

I know that I'm not a special case: a lot of folks in this downturn economy have had to leave their communities under pressure, and feel displaced in many of the same ways my family and I did. Great numbers of people have lost their jobs, and lots more will. They have to go wherever they can to earn a paycheck. Moving is never easy, even when it's a hopeful move; and moving from a place where you feel deeply connected is documented as one of the most stressful things humans can do. Many people report feeling depressed for months—even one or two years—following a move. Some people become clinically depressed. We did not experience this, but my wife and I might have, had we not intentionally helped others as a daily way of life. The facts are clear: such moves rank just under the loss of a spouse as among the chief causes of stress in America, and we are a nation where displacement is the norm for a great many people. We do not give community and stability of place their due. We are always feeling like resident aliens in a strange land, and are slow to realize that we are creatures who need stable places in order to stay well. The philosophers, like Stony Brook's Ed Casey, have a term for this need: *embodied implacement.*[1]

A number of studies show that when a middle-aged person relocates after laying down roots and becoming part of a social fabric, it takes about eighteen months to adjust and feel normal again; and in many cases, it is really a few years before folks feel fully at home. In retrospect, this was pretty much true for me. For some people it takes less time, and for others a lot more. Some never adjust, and they are unhappy for years. In the literature, the process is usually associated with a period of deep grief that eventually subsides.

Social integration—feeling that one is part of a community, rather than feeling isolated—is a well-accepted key to mental and physical health. More than ten major longevity studies have shown that people who are socially integrated tend to live longer. According to Robert D. Putnam's book *Bowling Alone: The Collapse and Revival of American Community*, over the last couple of generations we Americans have lost much of the social glue that once connected us, and we are in danger of becoming a nation of strangers.[2] Social connectedness has been a topic related to health since the nineteenth-century sociologist Emile Durkheim wrote his classic work, *Suicide*. Suicide is very rare in tight-knit communities, more common when connectedness is disrupted. Putnam summarizes the health literature with accuracy: "The more integrated we are with our community, the less likely we are to experience colds, heart attacks, strokes, cancer, depression, and premature death of all sorts."[3] We Americans have possessions galore, but our health is not dependent on what we have so much as on how we live. My heart really goes out to people who are part of companies that require a lot of moving, as though we humans can easily leave one set of friends and circumstances and connect with another whenever necessary, over and over again. We need community, and we need to value community more than we do. The myth of possessive individualism is the beginning of much literal illness.

Displacement is stressful for most people unless one is a natural wanderer who just does not dig roots to begin with, or such an extrovert that rebuilding a social world is as easy as pie. Over the last thirty years, more than a dozen large population studies from different parts of the globe show conclusively that people who are disconnected from others are two to five times more likely to die of all causes when compared to people with close family ties, friends, and community. They have more problems with sleeplessness and are less happy than the socially connected.[4] If you have the choice of moving or staying where you are, don't move before you've really thought it through. If you have no choice in the matter, be aware that you will feel displaced, and treat yourself with great care. And whenever you meet someone who has just moved into the neighborhood, reach out and be a good neighbor. Hospitality to the "stranger" is a precept as old as the Hebrew Bible. It is especially important because folks on the move are vulnerable. Hospitality creates a friendly space where strangers can enter and find safety.

Big moves—of any kind—require so much soul searching! We all ask a set of similar questions. Who do I want to be? How loyal are we to this place? How do I want people to remember me? Are we going to be happier? Is there a time to move just to not get stuck? Am I abandoning a place and its people? Am I making this choice in resentment or fear? Will I ever get another chance? What impact will this have on my family? Am I willing to take the risk? And once the decision is made and we say, "Of course this was the right thing," at some level we still ask, "Did I really do the right thing?" And the answer can only be, "Well, time will tell, eventually." See, the trouble with life is that you never really know.

What about our health? Family ties, friendship networks, and affiliations with religious groups and social organizations are among the connective tissues of a healthy life. There is absolutely no controversy over these sorts of facts. They are accepted by scientists around the world. Isolation kills, plain and simple. And when we leave a whole lot behind at many levels in a big move, health and happiness are put at risk. I knew these facts cold, and had attended some of the major conferences on social capital theory and health over the years. But still, we had to make the big move.

So it took quite a while to adjust, but with time things did grow easier for all of us, as one would anticipate. We still missed Cleveland, but we learned that yes, we can move and live through it. Stony Brook University is a great and challenging place full of good and smart people. Mitsuko loves her job, she found a good friend, and she's close to Edgewater, New Jersey, for her Japanese shopping at Mitsuwa. Andrew began to become more comfortable with New York, adopting the Yankees as his hometown team. (Of course to Cleveland Indians fans, like myself, the Yankees are the sports equivalent of the anti-Christ.) The Indians lost a fan, but I was relieved that Andrew adjusted as quickly as he did. He is an extrovert for sure, and has a strong personality.

Yet when you lose the very ground of your being because of decisions made by powers outside yourself, as we did, you experience unambiguous grief. Life suddenly seems both very hard and very fragile. Tensions grow; stress mounts. Ultimately, the experience taught me that bonds of affection, good neighbors, and ultimately, love itself are the most essential things in a happy life. Much is gained and lost in a big move, and it was pretty clear that we had to recreate what was lost as quickly as we could.

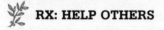 **RX: HELP OTHERS**

So with this move, no matter how I really felt, I mindfully kept a kind heart. We began at home, helping our son adjust to this enormous change in his life. Mitsuko helped her students tangibly, every day. The atmosphere in any medical school is not uniformly upbeat and chipper, so it was my task to uplift people, and I found a lot of meaning and satisfaction in this task. I consciously tried to listen attentively to everyone and treat people well. At the time, I was doing a little guest lecturing for the Masters in Applied Positive Psychology at the University of Pennsylvania, so I delighted in this little experiment of trying to create a positive psychology in my new workplace.

Each morning I would ask myself, "How can I best love the people I will encounter today?" And I would envision them, their needs, and how I might be supportive of them. Prayer was important. When we visualize things the way they should be, it quickens our resolve to be of benefit to the people around us and moves us into that state of being I call the "giver's glow." Altruistic, loving prayers and meditations are clearly good for those of us who engage in such practices. They galvanize our intentions to enhance the lives of the people we encounter. Around the office, the university, and the local community, I tried my best to serve folks and be supportive of them, and this made things a lot better for everyone and for me.

Although we didn't call it "workplace spirituality," that's what it was. In fact, my best helper, administrator Elisa Nelson, and I have some common spiritual commitments around hospitality and self-giving. We found such value in this. And Iris Granek, the chair of preventive medicine, led a small group in self-awareness with meditation. Together, we created an atmosphere of inclusive spirituality, and that made a big difference.

I also began studying moving from many perspectives— theological, philosophical, political, psychological, epide- miological, sociological, and medical. My work benefited, and

I think I became a more sensitive person in the process. I'm not a proponent of suffering for the sake of suffering, but in my case it became an opportunity to grow.

🌿 HEALING IN PLACE

Esther Sternberg, one of my friends at the National Institutes of Health, is a world-renowned scientist who studies stress and emotions in relation to illness and health. Her book *Healing Spaces* is an elegant scientific statement about how important these spaces and places are to happiness, health, and healing. The right vistas, the right sounds, the right architecture, the right colors all have a proven impact in lowering stress and enhancing psychological and physical health. When we are feeling particularly stressed, we can visit such spaces to be alone, to listen to God, to hear the words our own souls are speaking.[5]

We attend a church on Sundays in the village of Setauket, but I try to find sacred spaces everywhere. Stony Brook University is a great school, but it has none of the glorious old sacred spaces that one finds at universities with religious histories, even if they have turned secular over the years. There is no Riverside Church on the street corner like Columbia enjoys, no Rockefeller Chapel like we had at the University of Chicago. If someone from the university passes away, there is no sacred space on campus to have a memorial service. Historically secular schools like MIT have wonderful interreligious chapels that have been built in recent decades to provide students, faculty, and staff with a sacred space, and perhaps all schools will someday follow suit.

Fortunately for me, I discovered in the university hospital a small chapel about twenty feet square where people of all faiths can bring their spirituality to a quiet place and pray for their loved ones who are ill. To me, it feels like the one spot that is honest about human spiritual needs, and I stop by for just a few minutes on the way to my office most days. Maybe it is only in environments like hospitals, where people and their families are dealing with life and death, that the well-nigh universal call of spirituality must be more openly acknowledged.

Nature, especially, is a good place to find your sacred space. In the historic Stony Brook Village, just past the old duck pond off Route 25A, lies the Paul Simons Nature Preserve. Up the wooded path at the top of a hill sits a beautiful labyrinth where I like to go sometimes to reflect on whether I have been treating difficult people with a healing attitude. On the edge of the labyrinth sits a large rock, about fifteen feet high with a flat vertical face. Climbing up that face is a life-size metal sculpture of a young man, his feet and fingers gripping into the stone where it seems there are no safe or obvious holds to welcome them. The flat rock surface always seems ready to throw the young man off.

I resonate with that young man. It seems as though life is always trying to throw us all off, to let the force of gravity drop us on our backs into the dust of the earth from which we came. Moving put me and my family on the face of a rock for a while, just hanging on. The nature preserve became a sacred space to me, a place to pause and reflect. I treasure it to this day and walk the paths of the preserve when I get the time.

I found one more sacred place on the ferry that goes across the Long Island Sound from Port Jefferson to Bridgeport, Connecticut. Every month or so, I just like to jump on it and go for a ride. I don't actually get off the ferry because Bridgeport is not exactly a tourist attraction—although I am sure that for many people it is a wonderful home, just as Cleveland became for me. No, I just stay aboard, drinking some tea and having a little Drake's coffee cake, watching the waves and doing some writing. (I have been eating Drake's coffee cakes since I was a little kid.) The round trip takes about two hours, which is a nice amount of time to connect with the sea and get away. Also, because I don't get off, I only have to pay the one-way fare. So this just costs me about $20, a fair price to spend for a day hanging out with the gulls in the fresh sea air.

The ferry reminds me that where we are now is not where we are always going to be. Life is a journey for everyone, and journeys never end.

❧ A DEEPER SPIRITUALITY

I think about things like God's will and its role in how we come to make our choices in life. People often assert, "I know God has a plan." I believe this to be true based on scripture and experience. God has an unseen hand moving behind the scenes of our lives. We are given a good deal of latitude, and when we make mistakes or are adversely affected by the actions of others, the messes created are not the last word. The worst thing is never the last thing, and adversity is also opportunity. In any situation, no matter how difficult, we are what we think. Every thought we allow and each word we speak literally creates the world around us. "Where there is no vision, the people perish" (Proverbs 29:18). I am a hopeful person because I do not see that one really has a choice about the matter. We either hope or die, it seems.

Faith matters for me. In fact, through this move from Cleveland to Stony Brook, I have become deeper spiritually. Never has worship, prayer, or doing "unto others" meant more to me than in the context of this move. These have been my emotional center, the place from which creativity, hope, persistence, humility, and love flow.

Love may not be just something between people, but a palpable force that flows from the universe, through us, ever outward. Like many people, I remind myself of this intuition through a daily spiritual practice. When I rise in the morning, which is usually about five, well before quietness gives way to the rush of human activity, I pray and visualize for a bit, usually while sitting or lying down. First, I just concentrate on my breathing and relax. Then I imagine or visualize the events of the day that lie before me, being thankful for all the good things as if they had already occurred. Call this a mental dress rehearsal. It is so important not to be racing around doing things all the time. We need to take time to be grateful for our very being, and to center our emotions and intentions on doing "unto others" in concern and affection. I know that this may seem like an awful lot of time devoted to spiritual exercise, but it actually seems to slow down my life, giving me more time that is less harried. From this strong, quiet center I become the kind of person who can change the spirit of my environment for the better and create the kind of contagion that allows other people to live better. When I fail to pray and visualize, as can occur on a very busy morning when I have to rush too fast to get started in the right way, the day never goes quite as well. The meaning of life seems to get away from me because I lack focus on it. Intentionality is crucial.

As one who had been much involved in research on spirituality and health for two decades, I know that this prayerful centering on the love of others lowers stress levels, helps with immune strength and healing, and prevents depression. We will never know what such practices do for the ones we pray or meditate for; but for the one who prays or does what my Buddhist friends call "loving kindness meditations," this centering on others rather than on self provides the altruistic orientation to life that is genuinely healthy. We know this from compelling studies of Buddhists who do "loving intention" meditations for others, and we know it from studies of Christians in altruistic or "intercessory prayer" for others. These benefits do not seem to occur if our meditation and prayer are centered on ourselves and our own wants and needs.

 **FORGIVENESS**

During those first hard months, as my son and I drove back and forth from New York to Cleveland along Route 80 in Ohio and Pennsylvania, I couldn't help but think about the Amish, whom we would glimpse from time to time in their horse-drawn carts, or working in the fields. The Amish live in a community in which forgiveness is such a core practice that apology is unnecessary. Of course, we all need to forgive and be forgiven to get through life every day.

I recalled giving psychiatric grand rounds lectures at Penn State Hershey Medical Center two days after a thirty-two-year-old milk truck driver shot ten Amish schoolgirls in Nickel Mines, Pennsylvania, on October 2, 2006. The gunman took ten young Amish girls hostage, sending all the adults out of the building. The police arrived quickly, but before they could act, the gunman had killed five of the girls and wounded the five others with shots to their heads.

On the very evening of the crime, the Amish went to comfort the killer's family; days later, they attended his funeral. Then they razed the schoolhouse with bulldozers, and in a wonderful communal rite of passage, they built a beautiful new schoolhouse over the course of a few days. It helps to have a community in which forgiveness is encouraged and supported.

The girls were flown into the Hershey Medical Center, which is the trauma center for Lancaster County. I was there, two days after the event. People in the hallways everywhere were shocked and in a state of silence. In one of my seminars for clinical pastoral care, nearly all the pastors were in tears, but they were also inspired by the Amish traditions and wanted to become better forgivers and reconcilers themselves. The Amish became a model for me then, and I called on that experience as I struggled to forgive my former boss for what I realized was a much smaller loss than the one the Amish had forgiven immediately with elegance and grace.

Forgiving is more complex than giving. We can forgive with tender hearts, but we must be tough minded in order to ensure that destructive behaviors do not run rampant. We become enraged, but forgiveness prevents rage from becoming demonic. Forgiveness is only possible through love. It is the power of love that best pushes aside our bitterness and lifts us above our miseries.

Holding grudges is a terrible way to live. It saps all the positive energy from life and drives us into an emotional dungeon. Nothing interferes with creativity and good judgment more than bearing grudges, and few things have destroyed more otherwise good and promising lives. Forgiveness, difficult as it may sometimes be, makes us stronger, wiser, and happier, no matter what we have lost. From a Buddhist perspective, forgiveness is always possible, and we should forgive always. As Matthieu Ricard has written me, "hate devastates our minds and causes us to devastate others' lives. Forgiving means breaking the cycle of hatred." The Buddhist believes that the basic goodness of a human being "remains deep within, even if he or she deviates into a very malevolent person." Ricard, an esteemed Buddhist monk of French origins who lives in a monastery in Nepal, underscores that "love is the ultimate weapon against hatred." No doubt, there were a few days when cultivating love was my ultimate weapon, and my ultimate enemy was not that someone who had made my life more difficult, but rather hatred itself. It is like acid on metal over time.

Forgiveness, for me, is one spoke on the wheel of love. Love, an affirmation of the life of the other, and a willingness to participate in that life, is a basic disposition of the self that precedes any of its practical manifestations. Sometimes, we love others *in spite of* themselves, overlooking things in them we do not find appealing. No one has to earn this love. It is a love of radical and "unlimited" acceptance, even if it is also tough love. And sometimes we love *because of* something in others that is appealing. Most of us love people both in spite of and because of themselves, and we hope that those who love us will find at least something special and appealing in us. In real relationships, love is a mix of *in spite of* and *because of*. So maybe we are always forgiving people a bit. If we weren't, we would live in isolation.

The hardest form of forgiveness is self-forgiveness. People have to live with themselves. The trouble is that we are never good enough to really live in comfort. There is that passage from the New Testament, "Call no one perfect." So I have to lean on having already been forgiven by a God with a bigger heart than we might think possible—a God with a love that accepts us when we cannot otherwise accept ourselves.

ALWAYS SOMETHING NEW

If we hadn't applied the helper therapy principle, this move would have been so much harder than it was, and forgiveness and self-forgiveness would have been tougher. Helping truly does help the helper. Although none of us would have chosen to leave our home and friends in Cleveland, we've all found hidden gifts in this move. Andrew learned that he is a strong, resilient person who can make good friends wherever he goes. Mitsuko and I have also settled in, exploring and embracing our new community and continuing to make new friends. And although we know that deep relationships are built over many years, we have begun sending new roots deep into the soil of Stony Brook and Setauket. I guess we've all learned that we're stronger than we thought we were, that we can find happiness and peace in this place too. Sometimes it's right to be where we are most needed, where we fill the biggest void, and where we can be uncomfortably pushed to grow beyond our comfort zones to once again appreciate the journey. In the Hebrew Bible, people are often pulled out of comfortable places for good things that their limited minds cannot even begin to comprehend at the time. This is what Exodus is all about. Certainly, I reconnected with the fundamental biblical truth that we cannot see ahead well enough to know how, in God's hands, disaster contributes to destiny, and that God's love can reach down and use even our worst moments for good. Romans 8:28 puts it this way: "And we know that all things work together for good to those who love God, to those who are called according to God's purpose."

In the meantime, we can experience joyful moments, know that we can live through the difficult times, and have confidence that we are also being trained for something to be later revealed. Like children finding Easter eggs in the weeds, we can find the hidden gifts of giving, happiness, compassion, hope, and unlimited love amidst the stormy, rock-strewn paths of our most troubled times. We may flounder a bit on big moves, and even feel a little dazed and confused for a while. Like the man eternally climbing that impossible vertical rock face in the Paul Simons Nature Preserve, we may feel in danger of slipping, and we may even fall. But with time, unceasing prayer, and God's love, we can regain our balance and continue on our journey, always moving toward something, always arriving at something new.

James Joyce wrote, "To live, to err, to fall, to triumph, to recreate life out of life." We had not erred necessarily, but we did have to "recreate life out of life."

2

The Gift of the "Giver's Glow"

About five months after our move to Stony Brook, settling in to my new work but still struggling to deal with feelings of displacement and loss, I ran headlong into the holiday season. I missed our friends back in Cleveland, our church, the small traditions we'd established over the years. Although our Christmas mantel was decorated with many cards from friends who I know truly did wish us a happy new year, I found myself feeling a bit quiet when all I wanted was to enjoy the holidays. Then one of those serendipitous moments came along that refocused me toward what I knew to be true: that the hidden gifts of helping would far outlast the other gifts these holidays might bring.

During a December train ride on the Long Island Railroad, traveling back to Stony Brook from a meeting in Manhattan, I fell into conversation with my seatmate, Jack, an amiable man some years older than myself. In the sudden intimacy that can arise between strangers who know they will never meet again, Jack told me that his wife of twenty years had divorced him and that he had been fired from a job he'd held for thirty years, was newly diagnosed with cancer, and was close to running out of his retirement savings because he'd had to spend the money on day-to-day living. The one thing that was holding him together through all this, he said, was a volunteer job he had serving meals at his church's soup kitchen in Port Jefferson. "It's not just that I can't feel really sorry for myself when I see so many others who have no resources at all," he explained. "When I put that food on their plate, and I know they're really hungry—they can't just run to the fridge, like I can—I can see that I'm really helping someone. Even if they're too exhausted to acknowledge me or say thanks, that's okay. I don't know," he shrugged, "it just makes me feel like I can keep going another day, and things might start to get better. It's odd, but some days I feel better than I ever have."

"Thank you." I felt as if I had been jolted awake from a deep sleep.

"Sure," he said, clearly confused about what I was thanking him for, and why I was smiling. But I felt as though I'd just been handed my first real gift of the season. This man had far more reason than I had to be suffering the holiday blues, yet by sharing his story he had helped me let go of some of my concerns and remember what I already knew: when all else fails, we can still give to others. And doing so will always be our salvation, our reconnection to the world. This phenomenon of "the giver's glow"! I have learned never to underestimate its power.

You've probably seen people waving brightly colored glow sticks at a nighttime event, and you may have had the pleasure of experiencing the magic of snapping the tube and seeing it suddenly light up, creating a soft, colorful glow that lasts for hours and can light your way on a dark night. The principle is simple: the chemicals in the translucent plastic tube mix to create the glow—but *only* when you break the tiny glass capsule inside the tube. The brokenness is part of the process, just as the broken parts of our lives can allow us to reach out to others and create radiance, lighting the way not only for those we serve but also for ourselves and everyone we meet. The amazing thing is that with advances in brain scan technology, we can now begin to understand this glow at the physical level and measure it with biological markers. When we help others, we are tapping into a caregiving system that involves the brain as well as hormones.

Mitsuko, Andrew, and I all agree that the lowest point of our lives came a few days after we had left Cleveland and landed on the rocky Long Island shore. We were spending a few nights at a hotel in Stony Brook Village while we waited for the movers to arrive with our worldly goods. We were crammed into a little cottage that felt old and cold because it was. There were two beds, a few old bits of furniture, and a drab bathroom, and it was thunderstorming and utterly dark outside in the early evening. This was the perfect place for all hell to break loose, and it did. The enormity of this move began to sink in at a really deep level. Andrew started yelling at me, as kids do, and Mitsuko was crying out in tears, "I can't believe this! What a total disaster!" I was the least popular husband and father on the face of the earth. I said, "Let's give it some time; things will work out," but my credibility was at an all-time low. I needed hope, which is wrapped up in faith, because mere optimism was too superficial and was clearly not going to do the trick. I took a drive on my own for a while, and after I returned, Mitsuko and Andrew were asleep. I tiptoed quietly.

Fortunately, the movers came quickly. A few days after we moved into our new house, Mitsuko went across the street to the local elementary school, where she found a position helping first-graders with behavioral or learning problems. She was assigned a student who was especially cherished, and who presented behavioral issues during the course of the day. Mitsuko spent the next nine months with this little girl, helping her throughout the school day. It was often challenging, and there were more than a few evenings when Mitsuko felt exasperated. But she found great meaning in this way of helping. And in the evenings she would make beautifully creative origami gifts for the children in her class, illustrating for them the characters in stories the students were reading as a group. Mitsuko put so much work into these wonderfully elaborate posters and cards and illustrations that it astounded me. But this was her way of giving, through creativity; her hands were at work crafting things in the spirit of love. More than once, she's told me, "I cannot imagine how I could have survived without those kids."

For Andrew, the transition was a jolt, and he let us know it. He wanted so much to start school with his old friends in Shaker Heights, but he couldn't. The day that middle school started in Cleveland without him was a rough one. And on his first day at the Gelinas School here in Setauket, we couldn't say a single word to Andrew because it was so hard for him as he reluctantly left the house for the bus. Andrew was the new kid, and he had no friends. He knew no one. "That morning," Mitsuko remembers, "he looked really sad and was speechless. But that afternoon he came home and said, 'Mom, I had a very good day. Ten people, including girls, wanted to have lunch with me at the same table.'" That was joyous! And a few days later, our son adopted a new name the other kids had started using, "Drew," and he asked us to start called him that too. He was reinventing himself. Drew is definitely an extrovert, and this allowed him to connect with new friends quickly.

I also began to connect with my new colleagues. Mitsuko began to connect beyond the children, with teachers and parents and the larger community on our little island. The new Drew, with the resiliency of youth, continued to make friends, and began a transformation that continues to amaze us. Together, we helped each other recreate our lives.

🌿 HELPING OTHERS MAKES US HUMAN

Here's the recipe for living a rich, less stressful, healthier, and more meaningful life than you thought possible—even if your world has been pulled out of midwestern earth and transplanted on an island: give of yourself to someone else. Even the smallest act is healing. In fact, studies show that *just thinking about giving* seems to have a physiological impact.

In the 1980s, the renowned Harvard behavioral psychologist David McClelland discovered that Harvard students who were asked to watch a film about Mother Teresa's work tending to orphans in Calcutta showed significant increases in the protective antibody salivary immunoglobulin A (S-IgA) as compared to those watching a neutral film. What's more, S-IgA levels remained high for an hour after the film in those subjects who were asked to focus their minds on times when they had loved or been loved. McClelland called this the "Mother Teresa Effect."[1] There may be some alternative explanations, but the idea that tapping into the emotions of caring has an impact on biology is the most plausible and well established.

These researchers concluded that "dwelling on love" strengthens the immune system. And a growing body of rigorous research shows that generous people who frequently give of themselves to others live healthier, happier, longer lives than people who don't. Think about it for a minute: How could we humans survive without taking the welfare of at least some others as seriously as we take our own? We require the love and care of others, and we seem to have a profound, deeply evolved need for close, giving relationships. Parents are spontaneously generous and giving to their children, sometimes to the point of sacrificing their deepest desires and even their lives for them. Friends are also frequently generous with their friends, and strangers are often compassionate toward one another—as we've all seen happen with those everyday people who dropped everything in their own lives to help the survivors of Hurricane Katrina in New Orleans and those displaced by the devastating 2010 earthquake in Haiti. Something about moving beyond self and looking toward others brings happiness. When we stop expecting others to do things for us, and stumble on the happiness of doing things for other people, we can't help but realize that whatever happens, we can handle it.

We eat because it keeps us alive, and we help others because it keeps us human. This is what we are born to do, and the benefits are great—not only to those we help but also to our own emotional and spiritual well-being. Science tells us that there appears to be a fundamental human drive toward helping others. We prosper—physically, mentally, emotionally—under the canopy of positive emotions that arise through the simple act of giving.

Evolution suggests that human nature evolved in a manner that confers health benefits to the practice of benevolent love and helping behaviors. Well over a century ago, Charles Darwin, in his great book *The Descent of Man*, described in simple terms how compassion and generosity could have evolved so deeply into human nature that their inhibition would be disadvantageous: "For those communities, which included the greatest number of the most sympathetic members, would flourish best, and rear the greatest number of offspring."[2] Darwin, like David Hume and other philosophers who were keen observers of human motive and action, saw compassionate love as a powerful driving force in human nature. It makes perfect sense that if this disposition is selectively advantageous for group survival, there would be a related biological substrate conferring benefits on the giver. Today, a new science connects prosocial and giving activities with happiness and health, and we are learning more all the time.

HELPING IS BUILT INTO THE HUMAN BRAIN

Not too long ago, we thought of the body as a machine and the brain as some sort of computer that ran the show. But much recent research indicates that the brain is essentially a social organ with its cells and pathways wired for empathy, for experiencing the joys and sufferings of others as if they were our own. Our brain, our hormones, and our immune system are an intimately related care-connection system. Of course this system can be turned off by fear, vengefulness, anger, and other emotional states, but the care-connection system reasserts itself when these other states subside. The role of spirituality at its best is to gain self-control over the destructive emotions and to displace them in favor of sincere love of others. Spiritualities include sophisticated techniques of prayer, meditation, visualization, and positive affirmation that sway the balance toward living better.

The workings of this care-connection system are perhaps best described by the remarkable researcher Stephanie Brown, a colleague of mine at Stony Brook. According to a new theory that she and her father, psychology professor Michael Brown, reported in *Psychological Inquiry*, "The same hormones that underlie social bonds and affiliation, such as oxytocin, also stimulate giving behavior under conditions of interdependence." This action helps link those whose survival depends on one another.[3]

Giving and helping are wired into us, and our brains typically reward us with feelings of joy and satisfaction. How many times have people said that doing things to help others "just feels good," or that "I get as much out of it as they do." Researchers at the National Institute of Neurological Disorders and Stroke have worked with the National Institute of Mental Health and the National Institute on Aging on a collaborative project titled "Cognitive and Emotional Health Project—the Healthy Brain." The goal was to uncover the neurology of unselfish actions that reach out beyond kin to strangers. Nineteen subjects were each given money and a list of causes to which they might contribute. Functional magnetic resonance imaging revealed that making a donation activated the mesolimbic pathway, the brain's reward center, which is responsible for dopamine-mediated euphoria.[4] When people do "unto others" in kindness, it lights up the primitive part of the brain that also lets us experience joy. This is good news: even contemplating doing good for others goes with, rather than against, a big portion of the grain of human nature.

This system is deeply integrated into the human brain and human nature. Although we may have learned to think of ourselves as primarily rational and even selfish beings, science tells us that this simply isn't so. It seems we humans are as much *homo empathens* as we are *homo sapiens!* I strongly believe that in the next five years, most of the benefits of self-giving love and helping behaviors described in this chapter will be understood as a basic biological system. When this system is active, we tap into something vital that allows us to flourish.

Fortunately, activating it is easy: we just have to help someone. In a 2010 survey of forty-five hundred American adults, a good majority of those who had volunteered during the past year—a full 68 percent—reported that volunteering made them feel physically healthier.[5] In addition,

- 89 percent reported that "Volunteering has improved my sense of well-being."
- 73 percent agreed that "Volunteering lowered my stress levels."
- 92 percent agreed that volunteering enriched their sense of purpose in life.
- 72 percent characterized themselves as "optimistic" compared to 60 percent of nonvolunteers.
- 42 percent of volunteers reported a "very good" sense of meaning in their lives, compared to 28 percent of nonvolunteers.

Service is a key solution to many of the challenges facing this nation—not only new challenges brought on by the volatile economy but also the education, health, and environmental challenges we continue to confront. Fortunately, Americans are responding to these needs. According the Corporation for National and Community Service, key findings on national volunteerism for 2009 include the following heartening statistics:[6]

- In the midst of a lingering recession, 63.4 million Americans (age sixteen and older) volunteered in 2009, an increase of almost 1.6 million since 2008. This is the largest single-year increase in the volunteering rate and the number of volunteers since 2003.
- In 2009, the volunteering rate went up from 26.4 percent in 2008 to 26.8 percent.
- In 2009, volunteers dedicated almost 8.1 billion hours to volunteer service.

The challenges we face are bringing out the better side of Americans and slowly centering our attention on the things that matter most. As you will learn in this chapter, scientific investigations tell us that relatively modest activities—a few hours of volunteering once a week, or perhaps a "random act of kindness" a few days a week—help us live longer, healthier lives as they stimulate a shift from anxiety, despair, or anger to tranquility, hope, and warmth.

This feeling of elevation is sometimes described by psychologists as the "helper's high." At the psychological level, the helper's high was first carefully described by Allen Luks, who in 1991 surveyed thousands of volunteers across the United States. He found that people who helped other people reported better health than peers in their age group. This health improvement was set in motion when volunteering began. Helpers reported a distinct positive physical sensation associated with helping: approximately half of the sample said they experienced a "high" feeling, 43 percent felt stronger and more energetic, 28 percent felt warm, 22 percent felt calmer and less depressed, 21 percent experienced greater feelings of self-worth, and 13 percent experienced fewer aches and pains.

Most commentators on the helper's high believe that prosocial giving to others triggers the brain to release its natural opiates, the endorphins, but there is probably a lot more to this, including the involvement of such hormones as oxytocin, which causes the sense of calm in the helper's high.

Now, obviously not every helper feels this euphoria, so the glass is only half full. What can we do to fill it up more? Joseph E. Kahne and colleagues completed a survey of five hundred teenagers in the eleventh and twelfth grades and followed them for three years after graduation. Students found volunteering more meaningful and uplifting when they had forums in school that allowed them to talk about the social issues they were grappling with, such as homelessness and illiteracy.[7] Sincerity and good mentoring make a difference in the quality of any volunteer experience. Volunteers need to be well managed in meaningful venues that allow them to use their talents and strengths in order to be more effective, and it is important to let them select their preferred areas for volunteering.[8] There is a lot we do not yet understand about how best to organize, acknowledge, celebrate, and reward volunteers.[9]

I have spoken with several dozen teen volunteers over the years and conducted one survey. For the most part their experiences are positive and life changing. But there are always those volunteers who have been poorly managed, overwhelmed, frustrated, asked to do things they were uncomfortable with, or given leadership roles that they did not embrace. The more we enhance the organizational aspects of helping others, the more that people will experience elevated meaning and happiness uniformly.

🌿 THE HELPER THERAPY PRINCIPLE

I first heard of something like helper therapy from my Irish mother, Molly Magee Post. When I complained of feeling bored as a child, she told me, "Stevie, why don't you just go out and do something for someone?" Notice that she did not say, "Stevie, go read a book" or "Stevie, go clean up your room." I read a lot anyway, and kept an orderly room. So I would head across the street and give old Mr. Muller a hand raking leaves, or help Mr. Lawrence fix his mast. It always felt pretty good.

My mother's advice, which I have shared with others many times, turned out to be more fundamental to the course of my life than she had probably imagined. In fact, it has been documented that volunteering in adolescence enhances social competence and self-esteem, protects against antisocial behaviors and substance abuse, and protects against teen pregnancies and academic failure.[10] Simple chores—helping with the dishes, making one's bed, helping cook meals, doing laundry, and the like—are daily practices that make helping second nature. This kitchen table wisdom is the basis of scouting, Montessori schools, healthy families, and flourishing communities.

And, once again, science supports what we already know to be true. Adolescents who are giving, particularly boys, have a reduced risk of depression and suicide.[11] And giving during the high school years predicts good physical and mental health more than fifty years later, according to an ongoing study that began in the 1920s.[12]

The helper therapy principle can be a big part of the lives of recovering alcoholics. Both Bill Wilson and Dr. Robert Smith, the eventual cofounders of Alcoholics Anonymous in the mid-1930s, emphasized that the principle of alcoholics helping other alcoholics is, along with spirituality, the key to sobriety. The idea that helping others might have special therapeutic value was best articulated three decades later in 1965, in a widely cited article by Frank Riessman, the distinguished social psychologist and founder of *Social Policy*.[13] Riessman defined helper therapy on the basis of his observations of Alcoholics Anonymous and offshoot self-help groups that adopted AA's twelve-step program—groups that have involved hundreds of millions worldwide. Riessman observed that the act of helping another often heals the helper more than the recipient. In the early 1970s, discussion of the helper therapy principle appeared in the premier psychiatry journal. Scientists were observing the health benefits to helpers in a variety of contexts—including teens tutoring younger children.[14]

Recovering alcoholics since 1935 have practiced the twelve steps and noted the benefits to their lives. But the first empirical support for the link between helping others and staying sober first appeared only in 2004 in the work of investigator colleague Maria Pagano.[15] Using data from Project MATCH, one of the largest clinical trials in alcohol research, Pagano and her colleagues found that alcoholics who helped others during chemical dependency treatment were more likely to be sober in the following twelve months. Specifically, 40 percent of those who helped other alcoholics avoided taking a drink in the twelve months that followed a three-month chemical dependency treatment period, in comparison to 22 percent of those not helping. In two subsequent investigations, researchers demonstrated that 94 percent of alcoholics who began to help other alcoholics at any point during the fifteen-month study period continued to help[16]—and they became significantly less depressed.[17]

The use of the AA model by more than three hundred offshoot organizations—such as Al-Anon (for families and friends of alcoholics), Alateen (for children of alcoholics), and Narcotics Anonymous—is one of the great success stories of our modern times. Members use the power of their own experience and of their own wounds to lighten the burdens of others, and heal themselves in the process. They feel redeemed through helping others, move past shame, and accept new self-identities as role models. They are also attacking the narcissistic roots of their alcoholism. The benefits they receive in regard to an elevated recovery rate are most potent when they are helping other alcoholics, but the benefits are nevertheless considerable when they report significant helping outside of AA.

HELPING OTHERS IMPROVES MENTAL AND EMOTIONAL HEALTH

The benefits of helping others who have the same chronic problem as oneself extend to mental illnesses. In 2006, a major report on curing mental illness emphasized the role of helping others through involvement in mutual help groups. The report recommends this activity to people recovering from illnesses as disparate as depression and schizophrenia.[18]

This recommendation is encouraging, but it's something mental health professionals have long known. In some ways, it is reminiscent of the "moral treatment" era in the American asylums of the 1830s and beyond. Then, individuals suffering from "melancholy" (what we would call depression) and other ailments were directly engaged in helping activities for others in their therapeutic communities. Dr. Thomas Scattergood, a Philadelphia Quaker with a benevolent last name, and his colleague, Dr. Thomas Story Kirkbride, understood that contributing prosocially to a community of fellow sufferers would help the melancholic helper. The concept of helping others was put into practice as a treatment module by Kirkbride and other founders of the American Psychiatric Association, and has a place in the origins of American psychiatry.[19] The idea of the benefits of helping cannot be separated from the Quaker emphasis on benevolence.

Today, the therapeutic treatment of helping others is embodied by many mental health communities, such as the International Center for Clubhouse Development (ICCD) model, founded on the belief that recovery from serious mental illness should not be based on marginalization of the sufferer, but instead "must involve the whole person in a vital and culturally sensitive community. A Clubhouse community offers respect, hope, mutuality and unlimited opportunity to access the same worlds of friendship, housing, education and employment as the rest of society."[20] This model originated from the Foundation House in 1948 in New York City, and today there are more than two hundred ICCD clubhouses thriving throughout the nation as well as abroad. Lori D'Angelo, Ph.D., director of Magnolia Clubhouse in Cleveland, said, "I think that people tend to be more stable and happy if they feel like they are benefiting people more than themselves, or outside themselves. It helps them feel connected to a larger picture, and I would think that of human beings in general."[21]

HELPING OTHERS RELIEVES STRESS AND SOOTHES NEGATIVE EMOTIONS

A woman named Ilene recently wrote to tell me her story. It seems that she was especially caring and devoted while her husband was slowly dying of Huntington's disease, during what should have been the prime of his life. It was a crushing amount of stress for anyone to bear.

During that terrible time, "I had two choices," she says. "Remain miserable or do something good. I consider myself quite an optimist, and chose the latter." Interestingly, she was inspired by her husband, who had managed to stay positive throughout his prolonged illness, "right down to his last day on this earth. There were days that I would come to him with my own troubles, both out of a need to have this continued ability to share feelings with him to keep the intimacy in our relationship, and also because it really was difficult towards the end. Each time, he'd lift my spirits, even though I was there to lift his. I sensed that giving him the opportunity to comfort me actually helped give him some added sense purpose, as well."

While he was in the final stages of his illness, she said, "I also gave freely of myself as an alumni volunteer to my alma mater, Hofstra University. This helped counterbalance all that I was experiencing emotionally, giving me something positive to do to help others."

And after his death, Ilene continued to share her giver's glow.

Seeing there were no groups around for young widows and widowers in the area, I started one of my own: the Long Island/NYC Metro Area Young Widow/ers Group. This turned out to be one of the best things I have ever done. I'm continually helping others dealing with their situations, which is an uplifting experience for me as well. I've made many friends and also, in hearing their stories, I've gained a better perspective about my own situation. I realize I have many blessings in my life that others are not as fortunate to share. The amazing thing is, after only a short time since his passing, I find myself one of the most positive people I know, and my goal is to continue helping others around me also achieve this positive attitude.

In June 2010, I addressed Ilene's group in a restaurant gathering in Farmingdale, New York. They all understood from experience the power of coping with loss through self-giving. There was only one fellow there who disagreed. He said, "I never do something for nothing." I asked him if he was happy, but got no response. The group chimed in to support the role of self-giving in their own lives, but to no great avail. Some of us get so steeped in the ideologies of individualism that we become caught up in the idea that it is a bad idea to help others freely; this is just "a sucker's game," a "do-gooder's foolishness," an altruist's "self-neglect," or a way of encouraging "irresponsibility" in those whom we assist. This idea that helping others freely is for suckers does great harm to those who think this way, inhibiting the very capacity for self-giving that can bring them inner freedom and joy. I see it influencing the lives of those adolescents who seem to resist any display of kindness and are locked into an image of tough and clench-fisted indifference. These people are missing the best things in life. This crazy dualism of "I" versus "you" makes no sense.

Increasingly, the scientists are catching up with the giver's glow. The results of a recent bereavement study by my colleague Stephanie Brown and her husband, Dylan Smith, showed that people with a heightened stress response recovered from depressive symptoms more quickly if they helped others.[22] I have seen this often, so I was not surprised by the findings, but it's always nice when science backs up what you know to be true. It is a privilege to be working alongside these leading researchers. They also are working on research showing that dialysis patients who engage in helping behaviors experience less depression than those who do not.

Giving may be useful in ameliorating depression because it allows positive emotions like concern and compassion to push aside negative ones like hostility and bitterness, which take a toll on health. Science has long known about the connections between Type A personality, hostility, health problems, and early death.[23] Many have concluded that hostility is truly a health-damaging personality trait. Most researchers explain the increased mortality in hostile individuals from coronary disease and cancer on elevated levels of the stress hormones cortisol and adrenaline (also known as epinephrine), and a related lowering of the immune response, perhaps mediated by lowered serotonin levels.[24] So if you are the kind of person who falls heavily on the horn because the driver in front of you has the audacity to slow down at a yellow light, and you yell out some expletive in the bargain, you have a problem. Multitasking or being fast paced isn't what does damage; it is the protracted emotional hostility that creates a health issue for the heart. And the best way to turn this hostility around is to engage in doing "unto others" with helpful acts of kindness, reclaiming the heart at its best and for its best.

Although some studies have shown that certain kinds of low-level stressors may be beneficial to human health, the relationship between excessive stress and disease has been well documented. In response to such stressful emotions as rage or anger, the body secretes hormones that prepare it for physical exertion: the heart and lungs work faster, muscles tighten, digestion slows, and blood pressure goes up. These changes are good when we are running away from an attacker, but perpetually negative emotions eat away at us like acid burning metal. Negative feelings even slow down wound healing and are correlated with some forms of cancer.[25] In contrast, positive emotions can promote health and healing. When we reach out to others, our negative feelings of hostility, rumination, resentment, and fear are displaced by positive feelings of concern and love.

HELPING OTHERS MAY HELP US LIVE LONGER

Remember that saying "Only the good die young"? Don't be fooled into accepting its sad implications. I prefer to think of it this way: whenever we die, however old, we will feel young at heart if we live generous lives. In fact, the good actually die a bit *older*, generally speaking. People who volunteer tend to live longer, for instance.[26]

Longevity is the most studied physical health benefit derived from helping, and the findings are impressive. In a thirty-year study that began in 1956, Cornell University researchers followed 427 wives and mothers living in upstate New York. Women who volunteered at least once a week were found to live longer and have better physical functioning independent of baseline health status, number of children, marital status, occupation, education, or social class.[27]

But this is far from the only study. In their 2005 analysis of a nationally representative sample of 7,527 older adults from the Longitudinal Study of Aging, researchers Harris and Thoresen from the Center for Health Care Evaluation at Stanford University found that frequent volunteering was linked to longevity, and that giving to others—even if you're older, without friends and family, and in less than ideal health—can help you live longer.[28] They built on the work of Marc Musick, a professor of sociology at the University of Texas, and colleagues, who reported in the 1999 *Journal of Gerontology* that according to his research on elderly volunteers, "simply adding the volunteering role was protective of mortality."[29]

Doug Oman, a professor in the School of Public Health at the University of California, Berkeley, studied more than two thousand elderly residents in Marin County, California, over a seven-year period beginning in the early 1990s. He found that those who volunteered for two or more organizations were 63 percent less likely to die during the study period than those who did not volunteer at all. When Oman controlled for various factors—age, gender, number of chronic conditions, physical mobility, exercise, self-rated general health, health habits (such as smoking), social support (including marital status and religious attendance), and psychological status (for example, the presence of depressive symptoms)—he *still* found that the volunteers were 44 percent less likely to die during the time of the study than nonvolunteers. As it turns out, the likelihood of death during this period was more affected by helpfulness than it was by physical mobility, regular exercise, or weekly attendance at religious services. "If the present results are sustained," Oman and his colleagues concluded, "then voluntariness has the potential to add not only quality but also length to the lives of older individuals worldwide."[30]

An intriguing five-year study found that older adults who provided no instrumental or emotional support to others were more than *twice* as likely to die during those five years than people who helped spouses, friends, relatives, and neighbors.[31] It seems that it truly is better to give than to receive!

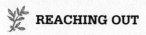 **REACHING OUT**

As my family and I made our transition to a new life in a new community, we realized that our choice was clear: giver's glow or doubter's darkness. We did a lot of little things every day to reinforce our giving practice, even just remembering to smile at those we met during the day.

Reaching out to help others saved my life, or so it feels. I know Mitsuko feels that way. "Every child is so special. Getting absorbed again in helping other children took my mind off dealing with my own difficulties in this time of adjustment. I had to look outwards, toward these kids, rather than looking inward at my own problems." I felt the same way, and with the astonishingly high quality of medical students at Stony Brook, this was easy to do.

For most of us, helping means being ready to lend a helping hand, or being willing to have our work interrupted when others need our time to make their lives a bit more manageable. This can occur in the family, in the neighborhood, in the workplace, in school . . . or just about anywhere. Recently, I received an e-mail from a woman who had been compelled to move from her country home to a city apartment better suited to her physical condition. Just before her move, she had some trees trimmed, separating a mother squirrel from her nest and scattering the babies. She gently gathered the babies, placing them near the tree, and watched until the mother returned to carry them one by one to an alternate nest. She wrote, "So, while I moved to another town, I came back to the house twice a week, called, "Momma! Momma!" and she would come to me . . . or, to the handful of walnuts I offered. This has gone on for many months, as I haven't sold my house. Believe me, I, too, get ample nutrition for my soul."

When I arrived at Stony Brook University, I was blessed to have a remarkable administrator as my right hand in all things. Elisa Nelson has been synergistic with me in every decision—without her, I would probably have perished grappling with the astounding educational bureaucracy. Elisa is one of the most diligent, generous, and spiritual women I have ever known. She was raised in a very distinguished Cuban family that had to flee during the revolution. Her mother worked menial jobs to raise her daughter, and she raised her magnificently as an exemplar of self-giving love. I could not have asked for a more perfect colleague for this project on compassionate care. Recently, the Face of America Project included Elisa in a commentary on its Web site.[32] Here are just some of the kind words they had for her:

> She is a giver, a helper, a doer of good deeds. In the time
> we were at the medical center, she helped us find a loca-
> tion for our shoot. She helped us fix a problem with our
> tripod. She saw to it that we had a quiet place for our
> interview. She made coffee for us. She introduced us to
> other staff members. She willingly shared her story with
> us. She volunteered to stamp our parking ticket. She
> took us to the cafeteria for a bite to eat, and she walked
> with us to the parking garage where we exchanged warm
> farewells.

Elisa is proactive, thoughtful and helpful in all the ways that matter. She is a woman of grace, dignity and humility who has mastered the art of selfless giving to others. Her face of America is one we will never forget.

So here's the recipe for a better life: enjoy being a generous, giving person and be generous and give often. The helping that goes on in everyday life, in the home, between friends, at work or school, or with a stranger at the food line is not what we would call heroic.

Here in Stony Brook, I kept it simple. I tried to be a consistent helper in small, everyday ways, even with just a bright smile and a hello. I accepted every little unpaid invitation to speak publicly at local libraries or volunteer events, and built up a presence in the local community.

One important practice for me was offering hospitality to my new faculty recruits. Each time we had applicants in, we really concentrated on making their stay an inspiring one. One of the best philosophers of altruism moved here from California, leaving behind many friends, good colleagues, and a developed reputation in the university community there. Three others came from Michigan. They all went through upheavals in relocating, just as I and my family had. Our empathy for each other helped us through the ups and downs of building a new program and rebuilding our lives.

Despite all our efforts as a family, we still had some bad days, some arguments, some sadness, of course. The stresses were unavoidable—that's the nature of moves. Yet by giving to others, we managed to keep our minds off our own issues (some of the time, at least) and that has helped heal us.

🌿 TAKE CARE OF YOURSELF WHILE HELPING OTHERS

But there can be too much of a good thing: "selfless" giving does not require you to neglect yourself! Giving is worth doing—but not to the point of exhaustion. Good people need to know how to draw boundaries around themselves so they can have time to take in nature, exercise, enjoy friends, and get away. Take the example of clergy members who feel the need to be available to congregants 24/7. Numerous reports indicate high burnout rates, and significant numbers end up leaving ministry because it gets to be too draining. Sometimes, when people feel called by God to do something, it is hard for them to acknowledge their emotional and physical limitations. Yes, we are one human family, and we are connected together in a common good. But we also need to learn to say "enough" and entrust others to take over for a while. I have known some really great doctors and social workers who have given their all to the neediest but did not know how to back off and find balance in their lives.

Please avoid the altruistic treadmill of doing more and more, running faster and faster. And don't compare yourself to others. Our need to give will vary at times and across circumstances, and we have our own unique physical and psychological limits. We all have certain fundamental needs to be loved and cherished, to be secure and respected. Helping others is not at all about getting rid of these needs, but rather about fulfilling the universal need to give and live better.

Balance is the key. At the right dosage, self-giving is a one-a-day vitamin for the body as well as the soul. We just have to be careful not to give away too much of ourselves in the process. We still have to look after ourselves, get some rest, eat well, and organize our lives to be effective in the long run. The last thing I want is for you to read this book and be inspired to run yourself ragged. Helping provides lots of hidden gifts for the helper, but do not exceed your capacity. Over the course of a lifetime, our giving can light many thousands of candles, but if our own wick gets too short through self-neglect, it can die out. Think long term, not like a sprinter.

One of the best ways to help others is by making it possible for them to step back and take a break. When I was just getting started at Case Western, I spent four years providing respite care one day a week for family caregivers of loved ones with Alzheimer's disease, just to give a break to people near breaking themselves. And it was certainly the most rewarding activity in that period of my life. But it was just one day a week. All these studies on volunteering and health describe "thresholds" of helping others that seem to create a shift in our emotional lives, but none of this research ever suggests that the more helping we do, the better we will feel. When it comes to cultivating generosity and kindness, however, do it all the time.

🌿 REPAIRING THE WORLD

Being concerned with the welfare of others simply has every kind of evolutionary advantage. Children do not thrive unless they feel cared for and experience empathy and loyalty. People in a particular group will prosper to the extent that altruistic emotions and behaviors like compassion and cooperation operate effectively. However we look at it, there are big advantages to helping emotions and behaviors. At the same time, it can be difficult to move from concern for our own group to concern for humans as a whole, for the "we" in the sense of a shared humanity. But that's where we can use spirituality and religion and also the power of the mind to move us away from the very shaky ground of thinking of ourselves as superior and others as inferior.

As a student of world religions and a Christian, I am convinced that when Christianity speaks of being a light to the world, when Buddhism talks about wholeness, and when Hinduism refers to the true self, at least part of what these traditions are talking about involves tapping into the euphoria, calmness, and warmth that scientists describe as an outcome of doing "unto others." This giver's glow has healing properties. Inner wholeness and true peace are related to the activity of self-giving love.

In the Jewish tradition, *tikkun olam* ("repairing the world") is thought to bring blessing and long life to the giver. It is through giving and helping that we lose our self-centeredness and gain a life energy that bonds us with others and with life itself. In support of this, Judaism also has a religious obligation called *tzedakah*. More than simple charity, it requires giving anonymously to unknown recipients, regardless of one's own circumstances. The Old and New Testaments both extol the rewards of giving: "He who refreshes others will himself be refreshed" (Proverbs 11:25) and "It is more blessed to give than to receive" (Acts 20:35). And the Dalai Lama distills thousands of years of Buddhist thought into this simple guideline: "Our prime purpose in this life is to *help others*." This is old wisdom, yet scientific evidence for its truth allows us to understand its depth better and take it more seriously as a way of life.

Whether we are looking at studies of older adults, middle-aged women, or preteens, we see that self-giving behavior casts a halo effect over people's lives, giving them greater longevity, lower rates of heart disease, and better mental health. This "kindness kickback" occurs partly because focusing on others causes a shift from our unhealthy preoccupation with ourselves and our problems, and it reduces the stress-related wear and tear on body and soul. It also seems to activate a part of the brain associated with joy, is associated with hormones that are linked to a feeling of inner calm, and even seems to provide a little immune system boost. Add to these biological benefits a more balanced perspective on our own problems and a greater sense of purpose, self-worth, and self-control, and wow! There is a real mind-body wellness upgrade.

Giving validates our own existence, and we can start right where we are. We do not need to travel far at all. Right here in this place is fine. We do not need to race around doing everything we can for others 24/7, as if the more we do the better we will feel. Helping others should be something about which we are all mindful on a daily basis. If we can hang on to the thread of self-giving over the course of a lifetime, this will create a glow of greater happiness and health over all that we do.

I cannot predict the future of the New York State economy or whether someday my status as a state employee will be threatened by big furloughs or layoffs. Nor can I predict how far housing values will fall, whether this will be a "double dip" recession, or if the burden of taxes will become even heavier. Things may get a lot harder in the United States as national debt goes through the roof and our children have to foot the bill. But come what may, we can all stay in close touch with the better angels of our shared human nature. This is where our strength lies. As Sir John Templeton wrote, "Every act of helping is a way of saying yes to life."

The Gift of the "Giver's Glow"   53

✿ FINDING YOUR OWN HIDDEN GIFTS
Giving

Giving to others, as should now be quite clear, has remarkable benefits for the giver. But it's not a cure-all—nothing is. It does not cure cancer, though I have known many cancer survivors who, feeling that they have been given a second lease on life, have devoted themselves to lives of amazing giving. It does not overcome aging and eventual death, though it seems to enhance longevity. It does not cure Alzheimer's disease, though love provides whatever resurrection-of-a-sort there can be in the lives of family caregivers and affected individuals. And people who are really deeply depressed cannot just "help" their way out of it; they generally need medical treatments first that will allow them to start to reach out to others.

Yet, regardless of condition, we can still give—whether it is a meal to a hungry soul, a hug to crying child, or a walnut to squirrel. You may not be able to trust that the world you have come to love will not shift beneath your feet, but you can trust your own heart always to reach out with love, even if it is just a matter of intentionally smiling.

Take a few moments now to think about how you can find the hidden gifts of giving in your own life:

• **Keep a journal about the large and small ways you are giving to people right now.** If you are having trouble thinking of any (I hope not!), ask a friend or loved one. You may be surprised to find that a friendly smile, a question about how things have been going, or an offer to pick up groceries helped someone through a rough patch and allowed him or her to keep going. Once a week, write down all the things you thought of, and discover how much you are already giving! Jot down how helping others makes you feel, in terms of meaning, joy, and health. Keep doing this for the rest of your life, whatever else happens.

- **Think about the ways others have given to you, right now or in the past.** You may want to give back to them with a simple, heartfelt thank you, or even a letter letting them know how much they helped you.
- **Visualize helping.** Every morning, take just five minutes to close your eyes and visualize yourself performing positive helping actions with some of the people you know you will encounter during the day—family, friends, coworkers, and strangers. Imagine a few specific interactions, including ones with the negative people you will inevitably meet. Use a little affirmation, such as "My words and actions heal." In psychology, this is called "priming." And there are lots of new neuroscience data to tell us why it is so effective in shaping behavior. You do what you envision, and you are what you think you are, all day long. If you do a little positive mental imaging before your day begins, you'll be more likely to respond helpfully to the world around you, especially in hard times.
- **Make it a practice to help one person every day.** This is an easy and gratifying exercise that with very little practice can become a natural part of your daily routine. It is simple to keep track of. Whether you help by holding the elevator,

dropping a dollar into a homeless person's hand, pitching in to help with a loved one's chore, accompanying a friend to a doctor's appointment . . . notice how this makes you feel, and write about it in your journal at the week's end.

- **Draw on your own talents in giving.** We all have special strengths and talents. You may love music, art, or writing; you may be athletic or mechanical; you may love reading and sharing what you've read; you may love cooking or sewing or any of the homely arts; you may be a computer whiz or a math lover. However great or meager your talent, as long as you're passionate about it, that's what counts. Research shows that we benefit most when we help others by drawing on our natural gifts—and they benefit too. Use the talents you possess. Develop them as far and as deeply as they will go in the service of others. People tend to stick with helping others when they are doing things that they feel they are good at.

3

The Gift of Connecting with the Neediest

Back in 1988, just after our arrival in Cleveland, I visited a nursing home in Chardin, Ohio, and sat down with a man named Jim. He was suffering from profound dementia, or from what can be called deep forgetfulness: he had lost most of that temporal glue that binds the past with present and future. I looked him in the eye, smiled, and called him warmly by name, asking him how his sons were doing. I knew that a verbal response was unlikely, and he could offer none. But he then he offered something much better! He placed a twig in my hands and smiled with a warmth and joy that lit me right up. He struggled to get out just three words, leaving me totally surprised. "God is love," Jim said. If love were electric, the room would have lit up like the Fourth of July. I returned the twig, and Jim wandered off.

The nurse who witnessed this told me that when Jim grew up on an Ohio farm, his father loved him very deeply and raised him in the Christian faith. Every morning, Jim had the same chore—to bring kindling in for the fireplaces. Now Jim had gone back into his past and found anew the time when he most felt the safe haven of fatherly love. That twig symbolized the love of his father and the joy that Jim felt in doing a small, helpful chore early in life. There, in the desert of deep forgetfulness, Jim was coping with the chaos of the present through his emotional memories of the power of love. He had enough security in this residual generosity that he could still relate to the world through giving. As he wandered off, I noticed that he picked up an old hand-sized puppet doll from the floor and actually walked over to a woman who was whimpering in the corner of the unit. When he placed it on her lap she stopped crying. Jim was a generous soul still, and I hoped that he would be able to keep it up to the end.

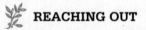 **REACHING OUT**

In this chapter we take the helper therapy principle a little further, casting the net more broadly to embrace some especially needful population that you feel called to help. This focuses our emotionally healing energies of self-giving love at a point of special calling. I discovered my own calling to work with the cognitively impaired when I was a student.

Mostly looking to find myself, I used to visit my grandmother at her nursing home. People did not use the word "Alzheimer's" back then, but just spoke of senility. Entering the nursing home, with all its odors and shocking sights, was difficult at first, but my grandmother still had a palpable warmth about her. She kindly offered me peanuts, forgetting that she had already sucked away the candy coatings from these once pristine M&Ms. I politely declined the peanuts, but I did read stories and poetry to her, and helped with feeding. She smiled at the sound of my voice as I read, and that mattered to me deeply. She was a teacher of love to the end, revealing that even in the throes of deep forgetfulness, love is a kind of resurrection. These simple actions of feeding and reading were the seed of the realization that sometime later in life I might be able to help others like her, and that's just what happened. In fact, in the early 1990s I started a number of poetry reading programs in assisted living centers for the deeply forgetful, who would sometimes surprise us all by chiming in unexpectedly with a verse that they had learned deeply, from memory earlier in life. They were especially able to chime in with the verse from popular tunes of their day.

Theology shaped my interest in the deeply forgetful. Why not elevate people who are cognitively disabled to a place of equal human significance and worth, and even allow them to free us hyperproductive, hypercognitive, and hyperrushed types from the crazy race of perpetual activity? Everyone knows that the weak of mind and the disabled need the help of the strong to get along from day to day, but not everyone realizes that the strong need the weak if they are to stay connected with the most essential features of being human—unconditional love, equal respect for all, and simply *being* rather than *doing*. I always enjoy saying to people with dementia something like, "Your life is just as meaningful now as it ever was." The moderately demented often enough surprise me with a response, such as "Thanks." Sometimes, but rarely, a person who is very advanced in the progression of dementia will surprise me too.

Back in Cleveland I had worked with the deeply forgetful for many years, both professionally and as a volunteer. I visited family caregivers, providing them with a chance for some respite. It meant a lot to them to get away for just a few hours once a week for a movie or a visit with friends. I also helped with the healing arts programs at a number of centers, using music and drawing in addition to poetry. All of this was a way of grounding a life of academic research and writing in service. From such beginnings in local helping, many good things would come, such as speaking and consulting on dementia care and ethics in more than two hundred cities and towns across the United States and Canada, and I wrote a book called *The Moral Challenge of Alzheimer Disease*. After 2000, I drifted away from this vocation, focusing more on the science of self-giving in relation to health and spirituality. But now, at Stony Brook, as I was teaching medical students about the benefits of compassionate care to their patients and to themselves, I began to feel that I needed to spend a little more time again interacting with the deeply forgetful, and decided to make more room in my life for active service with this population for whom I had a long-standing affinity. Maybe it would do me good to reconnect.

I started accepting invitations to speak in Canada, on the East Coast, and even in London. I spoke to large groups, spent one-on-one time consulting with caregivers, and responded to queries about various ethical and spiritual issues. There was for me a lot of benefit to assuming that familiar role. Maybe it was a way of asserting self-control in a new environment by doing a form of service that reconnected me to the Alzheimer's community. It was a great prescription for my own soul—good for them, I hope, but certainly good for me. At a two-day workshop in Hamilton, Ontario, it felt so good to be out there again with this amazing group of a thousand deeply caring family members and professionals that I felt ready to cry with joy. I found renewed meaning, and it certainly put in perspective my own suddenly less important problems.

With the clarity of my own displacement, I suppose that I could see myself a bit in these deeply forgetful individuals. They move to assisted living from a familiar home, and suddenly everything is unfamiliar to them. Competent professionals always recommend to family members that they move favorite pictures, blankets, objects, and other items of special symbolic meaning with their loved one. Why? Because science shows that the "symbolic self," the part of us that stays connected to the symbols that live in us as we live in them, has a great deal of staying power even very late in the progression of disease. The residents find so much solace in these symbols. I began to understand with renewed insight how symbols and familiar places and objects are a part of everyone's self-identity, including *my own*. And I began to think more deeply about that part of our human nature that is desperate to hang on to such things. The deeply forgetful find the world confusing because their memories are fading, and they live constantly in the pure present, the now. The best hope for the deeply forgetful is in the loving voices and warm facial expressions of the caring people around them. And in this, they are really not so different from the rest of us: they need to be loved, to feel good about themselves, to be respected, to be stimulated emotionally and relationally, to feel secure, to be included in activities, and to find moments of delight in the abundance of natural beauty. *They reveal these universal human needs to us who have forgotten them.* As I began to keep a journal again about the deeply forgetful, the challenges I had been grappling with subsided. I felt more like my old self again, part of a cause beyond self. People with all their faculties intact can find the world confusing, too!

And in the process, I was thinking about how love alone was saving me in this time of transition, and how its saves us all, just as it does the deeply forgetful. Life is often a very confusing affair, and we are all confused—just some more than others. We get off course, we make decisions for fool's gold, we say things we know we shouldn't, we forget the things that really matter and waste our lives. So in our confusion we need a perfectly accepting love, just as the deeply forgetful do. Because deep down, they are not that different than we are.

As I adjusted to my new job and location, I must admit that I sometimes relied on duty a little more than on my usual spontaneity. Fortunately—for me and for those with whom I came in contact—in my everyday life I had to reaffirm what I had always learned from the deeply forgetful and their caregivers: that love is the essential human reality. I wanted to be as accepting and generous to everyone as old Jim was when he handed me that twig.

There is so much loss and suffering in this world. When people become attuned to this, they are often overwhelmed by the enormity of it all and can become subject to malaise or even depression. They feel that there is no way that they can make much of a difference. In truth, suffering is everywhere, including in the affluenza of the north shore of Long Island. The best way to feel some effective agency and achievement in alleviating suffering is to focus in on that one population with which, over the years, you can gradually make a meaningful contribution. It is the experience of feeling that you can make a small difference using your particular strengths or talents that allows feelings of compassion to be constructive rather than overwhelming. I like to tell people that knowing that one can make a difference makes all the difference.

A MOVEMENT BEYOND SELF

Just as people living with dementia may find themselves lost in their own homes, we can wake one day to find ourselves lost in our own lives, made unrecognizable by the death of a loved one, a change in a relationship, a job loss, a financial crisis, or any of the slings and arrows life eventually throws at all of us. At these times, it's very easy to become preoccupied with our own troubles, feeling very much alone in our suffering and unable to break free of our own vortex of pain.

People speak often of what theologian Henri Nouwen called "the wounded healer": when we have ourselves experienced some particular form of suffering, we can empathize with others—we've been there; we know how it is. Much genuine helping in the world comes through wounded healers, everyday people who feel an urge to help others who are confronting challenges similar to those they once experienced and survived. Yes, we are hardwired for empathy with our mirror neurons and our caregiving systems, but these grow weak and can be easily overwhelmed by busyness, by negative environments, by having to please empowered people of malice who have the ability to punish. Love does take courage. And when we really identify with the needs of some special group, it is easier to defy the darkness.

At these times, the best move is one that takes you far beyond your own small world, to a needful group about which you have a passion. Here you have the opportunity to recreate community and connection, allowing new, deeper friendships that grow out of a common cause. It may be mentoring prisoners, as I used to do at the Grafton Correctional Institute near Oberlin, Ohio, or volunteering in a homeless shelter, or working with Mothers Against Drunk Drivers. It may be cooking or serving meals through a church outreach program for the poor, as the man I met on my train journey did, or participating in a group for widows and widowers, like the one Ilene started when her husband was dying of Huntington's disease. Or it may something quite simple, like knitting hats and sweaters for children with cancer, as my administrative assistant, Elisa Nelson, does.

Two years ago, Elisa joined a very talented group of women who share their time and talent by knitting, crocheting, and sewing handmade items for hospital patients who are required to stay for a long period of time—the premature babies who remain in the neonatal intensive care unit for several months after birth, the terminally ill adult or child in the intensive care unit, the patients in the surgical units, the lonely veterans in the veteran's home without family to visit them. "Each of us has a different talent," she says, "but we all have the same mission—to give to others."

The theory is that patients find great comfort in wearing a handmade knitted or crocheted sweater, being covered with a crocheted blanket, or hugging a soft hand-sewn pillow. In addition, patients simply feel better cared for, which helps the healing process. Patients and their loved ones welcome these gifts as signs of love and care from community members whom they do not even know.

"It is easy to give to our family and friends," explains Elisa, "because it is a natural instinct to provide for those we love, and to share our gifts and talents with them. I have knitted many sweaters, hats, scarves, and blankets for my family and friends. Most recently, I spent time knitting several pieces of clothing for my first granddaughter. But I did not feel the same state of bliss as when I give to those in need and unknown to me.

"An indescribable sensation comes over me when I think about the joy I will bring to a complete stranger with something I crafted with my own two hands. Sometimes when we give to others, our actions are tinted with the expectation of reciprocity. It is only when we give to others without strings attached that we feel as good as those who receive it. I take a lot of pride in knitting these items for the hospital patients, and knowing how much it means to the patients, I feel as if I just received a grand prize each time I give.

"The good feelings keep coming, though, after I finish knitting," Elisa says. "I am fueled with an incredible energy after I drop off the knitted items to the nurses in charge. I feel proud, not only of what I have made but for setting a good example. I feel renewed and more productive for the rest of the day. The more I knit, the more I give. The more I give, the happier I feel, and more important, the happier others feel. This is a great chain to be part of."

Or what stirs your heart may grow directly out of your life experiences, as it did for my friend Colleen Kelly. I first met Colleen in 2006, when she was a student at Kent State University and I was a guest lecturer on the philosophy and science of unselfish love. Colleen came to dinner with a small group after the talk, and was the most lucid and thoughtful young person I had met in a long time. Colleen has cerebral palsy; she has been wheelchair bound since childhood, and she struggles to do the simple things most of us take for granted. Yet Colleen is one of the most giving people I know. Now in her early twenties, she writes books, speaks to groups, and involves herself in volunteer work across Greater Cleveland. When I asked for her thoughts on the role of giving in her life, she wrote me this:

> I was the first person with a physical disability to enter my school system; the pioneer for other children like me to receive a better education. I was a senior in high school when I finally realized just what a difference I had made in the struggle for equality with regard to education for those in my school district.
>
> I was cruising down the hallway in my motorized chair when I was stopped by a woman that I didn't know or recognize. She waved me over, and explained that she was an interpreter for a deaf student. Then she continued, and said that it was because of me that her student was accepted into the high school. Her comment touched my heart, and for the first time I realized how satisfying it was for me to have made a significant difference in someone else's life.
>
> I remember a speaking engagement that I was asked to do for a class of second graders. It was a large group and I was sharing stories regarding my disability. I had just reached the part in my speech where I discuss how some people actually talk down to those of us with disabilities. Suddenly, out of nowhere, came a loud voice from the audience shouting, "I have to meet Colleen!" and again, "I have to meet Colleen!"
>
> A profound silence followed as I watched a small blind boy, guided by his assistant, walk slowly up to my

wheelchair. He reached out and touched my foot, my leg, and my joystick, and in that moment we understood each other perfectly. It was one of the most moving experiences in my life and I will never forget its impact! Here I was, sharing my story with a room full of children, hoping to give them an awareness regarding people like myself; people with disabilities. However, it was the action of the little boy that made the difference.

I like to think that I have helped others through my life experiences, but really what I have learned is that it is not what I have given to others at all, but what they have given to me! In each opportunity to give, there is an opportunity to grow. It seems to me that although giving gives us meaning in our lives, what we receive in return is far greater lessons in love and understanding.

So often our greatest giving is to people who struggle with our own challenges. A young medical student who discovers that she has the susceptibility gene for breast cancer begins volunteering in a support program for other women with this risk factor. Another, who grew up with a violent and abusive father who after many years was finally restrained, volunteers for a domestic violence coalition. Many of my friends over the years have been leaders in the movement to make life tolerable for those with developmental cognitive disabilities, such as those associated with Down syndrome. Most are themselves parents of children with these issues who have become effective advocates and champions for the rights of such individuals. These parents, who encountered every imaginable prejudice against their children, found their lives were empowered by devotion to this special cause that was close to their heart.

My friend Janet S, a former prisoner and recovering alcoholic, found her way to sobriety through Alcoholics Anonymous. She told me that every time she responds to a "twelfth-step call" to help other alcoholics in prison, she is profoundly inspired. Through serving this special population, of which she is a member, she found a salvation in her life that carried her through even the worst of times. Such service added meaning to her life, and a sense of making a difference. "I can do this!" she says. "I can really help these people and make a difference because I have been there."

Four years before he retired after thirty-eight years in the printing business, Ed Barrett decided to go back to school to study a topic that had plagued him for decades, the disease of addiction. "On the advice of a faculty member," he says, "I became an intern at Hazelden's New York facility and spent every weekday night counseling and running groups. Having completed the year, I went to Bellevue Hospital and completed another year of internship working with homeless men and women, and never left." He has been a volunteer for fifteen years, in places other than Bellevue. One of these is the Clinic in Phoenixville, Pennsylvania, which provides services to "working poor," many with both medical and mental health issues. Here is just one story of how his affinity for this group changed lives:

Many of our patients are unable to feed their families. The bad economy is destroying them. I decided to go into my neighborhood and ask for a modest donation on a weekly basis. I asked to leave one can of food that I would pick up every Sunday at their homes.

After a few weeks of knocking on doors the donations started to grow and my car started to fill up. Now people were leaving bags on their driveway and some started to ask if they could give clothes, then furniture. I would bring my collections into the Clinic every Monday morning on my way to Bellevue in New York. The patients at Bellevue for the most part have very few material possessions, but many have children and families. So, I started asking my neighbors in Philadelphia if they had any computers or TVs they didn't need, and almost every week I bring computers and TVs to Bellevue, where the patient government at the clinic decides who should get the items. In these transactions everybody wins. The patients at the Clinic in Phoenixville can feed their kids; the patients at Bellevue can give their families a computer to learn with and a TV for inexpensive entertainment. The donors have a sense of satisfaction of having helped another human being.

But the largest benefactor is myself, by having the privilege of being of service to my fellow man. And something interesting is happening. The patients are seeing maybe for the first time that someone cares about them. I believe if we think small, and see through the prism of compassion and caring, we can accomplish wonderful things for ourselves and other people.

Not too long ago, a number of great and giving medical students at Stony Brook University decided to form an a cappella singing group for the primary purpose of singing at events around the medical school, and to the hospital patients. Although none were professional singers—Kimberley Slonaker says, "I was a bit apprehensive . . . I had sung in a chorus in high school, but never without instruments"—they began rehearsing a variety of songs and playfully named themselves the Lymph Notes. Their experience has been a true and unexpected gift, for themselves as well as for the patients and their families. "I found myself surprised at how much our presence meant to so many patients," Andrew Mastanduono recalls. "I remember one woman in particular who seemed as if even moving her head would have caused tremendous pain; yet I could see her trying to snap her fingers as we sang a doo-wop song from the fifties. To be able to do something I love (singing) and for others to reap healing joy from that is truly amazing."

Lymph Notes organizer Esther Hwang says, "Before leaving the cardiac unit, we sang Gershwin's "Love Is Here to Stay" for a couple. The wife was sitting at her sick husband's bedside. As we sang, her calm face began to reveal sorrow, pain, love as tears trickled down her face, and her hands gripped her beloved's more tightly. I felt connected to her and privileged to experience her emotions with her. I also felt a strong tie with the Lymph Notes. Somehow, experiencing together the connection with others deepened our connection to one another."

The student singers speak of how even the most ill patients respond to their music, and how they hope that their medical careers will have the same kind of impact. Fiona Yuen says, "Currently, in pathology, we're learning about a lot of people whose lives cannot be saved by modern medicine, and I was starting to feel that nothing I could do or learn would make a difference. But singing today reminded me that even if we can't cure people physically, we can still help them enjoy their lives a little bit more."

One of the Lymph Notes, Alan Wei, wrote:

As a busy medical student, I easily forget to look around me at the many facets of patient care that transcend that which is physical. As we sang for patients in hallways of the hospital, the soothing sounds of an ensemble of voices in harmony meant much more than a song in itself. I was reminded that as a future health care worker, I could make a lasting difference in the lives of my patients simply by spending a few moments of heartfelt time to connect with my patients.

We traveled through various parts of the hospital from pediatrics and cardiology ICU to the oncology departments. A few moments truly moved me and reminded me of why I had chosen to pursue medicine. In the ICU, there was a frail old woman lying in the patient bed ahead of us. As we rounded up our positions in preparation for song, she stared at us with a gaze of curiosity that seemed to say, "Why hello! This is a nice change from the normal routine." As we sang the Del Vikings' "Come Go with

Me," her face lit up with a warm smile that wrinkled the corners of her eyes and made them sparkle. In an adjacent room, another patient tapped his foot in unison to the rhythm of our song. Through our song, I was touched by how we were able to connect with these patients and for a brief moment in time uplift their spirits.

On the oncology floor, I was nearly brought to tears as we sang Billy Joel's "For the Longest Time" for a middle-aged couple. The wife had heard us singing further down the halls and had asked that we sing for her and her husband. As I looked through the doorway, I caught a glimpse of the husband. He was seated upright in a hospital bed and appeared to be in a vegetative state with his head tilted slightly upwards and towards his wife. With one hand grazing her husband's cheek and the other caressing his hair lovingly, she looked into his eyes and whispered sweet nothings to him during our singing. In this profound moment, I felt that I not only shared an intimate moment with the patient, but also connected the patient with loved ones.

It is my wish that as I travel further along in my medical career, I remember these moments where the little things in the world make worlds of difference. Should I ever feel discouraged or overwhelmed, I will think back on these heartfelt experiences and remind myself of the greater meaning of taking an extra moment in the hallway to listen to a patient's concern, and providing my patients with meaningful ways to improve their lives and well-being. Through my experiences singing on the hospital floors, I have come to realize that we are humans who share more than the air we breathe and the planet we reside on; we are able to support each other through difficulty and weakness and connect with each other on a deeper level through our songs and emotions.

Whether your calling is singing, helping troubled youth, looking after abused animals, feeding the homeless and hungry, cleaning up the shoreline, working with the aged or children with special needs . . . Whatever your cause, embrace it now and share yourself with others.

THE SCIENCE OF POST-TRAUMATIC GROWTH

I recently performed a Google search for the term *post-traumatic growth* and was amazed by the hundreds of thousands of items that came up. In just a few years, this topic has really taken off. Post-traumatic growth refers to the sometimes profoundly positive psychological changes that can result from our struggles with challenging life circumstances. It's certainly not a new idea—the power of suffering to transform a broken or hardened heart is perennial. In life we are sometimes torn apart, and when with the help of time we are reconstituted, there is a higher degree of focus and purpose. Over the years, for example, in working with cancer survivors, I have noticed how often they want to use every day remaining to them to do good for others. And now science is backing up this intuitive truth. It helps to have faith that the hard times are trials we can use to shape mere optimism into deep hope, mere kindness into real love, mere happiness into real joy.

Individuals who face adversity often report finding benefits, and finding such benefits has been linked to psychological and physical health. Indeed, this became a focus of positive psychology with the publication in 1998 of an edited set of scientific papers titled *Posttraumatic Growth: Positive Changes in the Aftermath of a Crisis.* Very intriguing is the editors' statement that "Groups and societies may go through a similar transformation, producing new norms for behavior and better ways to care for individuals within the group."[1]

Traumatic events encompass everything from battlefield experiences to car accidents; from growing up in an abusive family to being the victim of schoolyard bullies; from discovering that a loved one is chronically ill to suddenly losing your job; from losing your life savings due to a bad economy to losing your home in a fire or flood. Traumas are unexpected, powerful, overwhelming. They shake our existential foundations and make us question all meaning and purpose. Sometimes, trauma results in post-traumatic stress disorder (PTSD)—a state marked by symptoms of irritability, depression, hypervigilance, exaggerated startle response, and other emotional and psychological issues.

But—and from this every one of us should take heart—trauma can also lead to PTG, post-traumatic growth. The "symptoms" of PTG include increased perception of competence and self-reliance, improved relationships with significant others, increased compassion and empathy, appreciation of one's own existence, changes in one's priorities, stronger spirituality, and a greater sense of meaning through love.

Let me share with you two wonderful passages from Psalms: "The Lord is close to the broken-hearted and saves those who are crushed in spirit" (34:18), and "He heals the broken-hearted and binds up their wounds" (147:3). PTG emerges out of the shattered heart. Those who move in the direction of growth accept their misfortunes and the idea that suffering can lead to growth; they affirm goodness and love as meaningful despite the dark night of their souls, and assert that life is worth living and that love makes it so; they have determination to make progress in the pursuit of meaning; they have confidence that even though all the evil is still there in life, they can make it through with *spirituality*, love, and the help and helping of others; they often develop a spirituality that involves some source of love in the universe that is mysterious and beyond self.

In life, we do not escape hardships. We can let those hardships destroy us, or we can discover new levels of endurance. When trusted friendships end in betrayal, for example, we can be thrown into unending gloom, or we can learn to filter out fair-weather friends and come to a deeper appreciation of those whose friendship is genuine. Adversity can devastate us, but it can also help us change our priorities and come to a deeper wisdom.

In the twenty years I have spent working with the deeply forgetful, I have met many friends. One of the friends I met along the way is Orien Reid Nix, the chair of the board of directors of the Alzheimer's Association. She grew up in Atlanta around the very spiritual African American thinkers, such as Benjamin Elijah Mays and Howard Thurman, whose work I had read and deeply admired in high school. She speaks of her experience of "love and the caregiver," rooted in caring for her own mother. She writes,

> Some call it a living funeral—a stunning, irrevocable event when the person you love, the keeper of all of your childhood stories, or precious memories that can only be shared between the two of you . . . are lost in the myriad of plaques and tangles of Alzheimer's disease. It steals much more than memories—it ravages everyone it touches, but what it doesn't kill is the immutable, indestructible *agape*—the unconditional love that is said to only be attributable to God—but I know is the one single force that drives caregivers to give every bit of physical and emotional energy they have to a loved one with Alzheimer's.

> And I believe that, even today, it is both my mother's love and my love for her that continues to drive me. As a chair of the association, there were many frustrating, difficult times, but I was always clear why I would never throw in the towel. I didn't when I took care of my mother, and won't start now. Everything I do today, all that I have ever and will ever achieve is because of the love, guidance and strength of both of my parents. They were exceptional people, and I have a legacy—a legacy of love that will never die.

In Orien's case, and for many caregivers, a sense of divine love as the background power and reality in the universe helped sustain her. I found this to be the case for thousands of caregivers I have met over the years. Indeed, in one research study, the spiritual sense that caregiving goes with, rather than against, the grain of the universe was the strongest predictor that a caregiver would get through the experience without suffering depression.[2] A spiritual sense of connectedness with divine love is no substitute for community support and respite, which are critically important, but under any circumstances, this faith in a love that is greater than our own helps immensely.

🌿 LOVE

Let me confess that I do not come naturally to the academic life, which sometimes seems to me to be a hypercognitive world one step removed from reality. Working with the deeply forgetful has always been my breathing space, a way to put service in the forefront, a welcome reminder that other ways of perception have validity equal to the intellectual.

I have seen caregivers of the most cognitively disabled help their patients find meaning and purpose in a warm and calm tone of voice, and a joyful facial expression that affirms the other. These caregivers make eye contact, talking with the person rather than around him or her. They validate the feelings of the deeply forgetful, and do not feel obliged to reorient them to our reality. They value the experience of being an attentive presence. The deeply forgetful, whose sharp awareness of emotional tones and colors shines through their cognitive decline, give me the gift of spiritual formation: for they respond to love, and love is their only resurrection.

And when I return to the world of the cognitively intact, this lesson spills over into all my interactions. I have a greater self-awareness of the potential impact of my words to uplift rather than put down. Thus, as I struggled to adjust to my new academic environment, with its intrigues, demands, and still forming relationships, a little work with the deeply forgetful centered my attention on what St. Paul called the greatest thing: "And now abide faith, hope, love, these three; but the greatest of these is love" (1 Corinthians 13:13).

THE SOBRIETY GARDEN

On my birthday, May 6, 2010, I made a remarkable discovery after giving a lecture at New York University for the Department of Psychiatry. Behind NYU's Bellevue Hospital lies an amazing garden about eighty yards long and sixty yards wide. It is called the Sobriety Garden, and it was started about twenty years ago by patients recovering from alcoholism and drug addictions.[3] The day I was there, many people, all recovering in some way, were out and about, planting and caring for what they were growing. This was a real community of growers, and they spoke of planting seeds in the ground as analogous to planting seeds of sobriety in themselves and in others. This was grassroots mutual aid and community self-help at their best.

These people knew well that their own health and success depended on their becoming role models for others struggling with exactly what they struggled with.

A man named James showed me around this oasis of peace and creativity surrounded by towering buildings. He took joy in every nook and cranny, replete with huge and wonderful sculptures, fabulous benches, charming pathways with careful stone inlay, and remarkably lovely gardens flourishing everywhere. He pointed out a young physician and her patient sitting on a bench under a pine tree.

This was a place where the hidden gifts of helping others just jumped off the page of life! This was my best birthday present in years, and I hoped that Willie Mays and Humphrey Bogart—who were also born on May 6—were looking over my shoulder at all this. And now I must confess the real reason that I wanted to visit the Sobriety Garden.

I grew up on Long Island on the south shore, in a town called Babylon. As I remember it, anyway, there was not much to do other than sail and drink. My parents were part of this culture as well, sailing and drinking. Sometimes Dad could easily down four or five drinks in the evenings after a long day working in New York City and the trip home on the Long Island Railroad, where many commuters already had drinks in hand. But Dad had grown up in this island culture, so he was its child. So much so, in fact, that when he was offered a vice president's position with Corning in the Finger Lakes area of upstate New York, he turned it down in order to stay by the shores of the Great South Bay that he loved.

I always felt that it would have been a good move, but Dad was nothing if not very loyal to the people he grew up with. In retrospect, I can see that maybe a big move would have been too much for him, but I also think that it would have been terrific for us all. Yet I do not think Dad ever viewed life as a journey. Life for him was in one place.

Thankfully, I somehow managed to break away from this pattern when I was fifteen. I was attending a boarding school in New Hampshire, following my brother's lead. Students were not allowed to drink, of course. But such rules don't always stop young kids from doing so, and on occasional long weekends, a group of us would go down to Boston and stay in the old Statler Hotel near Boston Commons, with the intent of drinking a bit much.

Then three things happened in quick succession that made me rethink everything. First, my uncle Gary Post, after whom I am named (my middle name is Garrard), died of liver failure in his early fifties after decades of clear alcoholism. At his funeral up in Connecticut, it occurred to me for the first time that people really harm themselves with alcohol. At the same time, I was hearing about my uncle Ray, on Mom's side of the family, who was a heavy drinker; he was spending his time on a houseboat in Dublin, Ireland, where he eventually drank himself to death. It struck me that I had a bad family history when it came to alcohol.

Then two close friends a couple of years older than I from back home got drunk, went speeding down the Montauk Highway late at night, ran their MG into a telephone pole, and died. This was really disturbing. Both were good athletes, good students, and nice guys. And people my age weren't supposed to die. Male teen drivers out on the partying scene have a high death rate. About that time my cousin Mickey, who had inherited money from the sale of a one-hundred-acre potato farm in Bridgehampton, squandered it all in a single year of partying and died on a night out when he crashed *his* MG into a telephone pole somewhere on the road outside the village of Southampton.

All of this came to a head when I was down in Boston at the Statler one Saturday night. I woke up early the next morning, in the bathtub. A very distinguished friend from New York's premier publishing family, who was emphatically *not* part of our little group, wandered into our room that morning. He looked down at me and said, "Post, can you do a little better than this?" Real friends are people who confront you when you are off track, rather than endorse your foolishness, and he was a real friend at that moment, though he may not have realized it.

I got up, appalled at myself and with a huge headache, and took a shower. Then I went off to a church across the street and determined never to drink again. It was a spiritual moment, and I never did drink again, even to this day. And when I got back to New Hampshire, I started volunteering as a tutor for French Canadian kids. Though never involved with AA, I think I sensed what the *Big Book* means when it says that "we" recover on the two axes of spirituality and altruism.

So from age fifteen I have kept on this track, sticking with a brain free of alcohol. I enjoy having a pure mind, a prayerful mind, and I really dislike big loud parties anyway. These days, one of the research projects I am most involved with is one headed by Maria Pagano, focusing on the role of service and helping others in teenagers' recovery from alcohol abuse. We have a national Web site (www .helpingotherslivesober.org) that presents our powerful research on how spirituality and helping others help adolescents in recovery,[4] and it is getting a lot of attention. I see myself in these kids, which brings me back to the point of this chapter: serve others who struggle with the same problems and issues that you have experienced in life.

Here in Setauket, I spend a fair amount of time driving Drew and his friends around and being a good role model for them, and I try to devote time to the undergraduate college at Stony Brook University that emphasizes community service. We see too many roadside memorials at the site of tragic accidents at telephone poles in our quaint village of Setauket. Drinking and related behaviors are the major cause of death in adolescents and college kids, as every trauma surgeon knows all too well. And increasingly, really good neuroscience shows that when kids start drinking young, before their brains are fully formed, it has a negative effect on certain regions of the brain as a long-term consequence. It also sets them on the path to lifelong heavy drinking and alcoholism. The studies are clear that a lot of adult alcoholics start drinking young.

For me, my family history was a clear red flag. I suppose that the best thing that happened when I decided not to drink was that I started studying spiritual classics and theology a lot more seriously, and it was then that I began contemplating how in the end it is God's love alone that can fill what Pascal called "the God-shaped hole" in our empty lives.

Just down the street from me there is a lovely park. It was dedicated to the memory of Frank Melville Jr. (1850–1935), the father of philanthropist Ward Melville, who restored much of the area. In my first weeks here, I found this poem inscribed on a stone bridge over a mill pond:

Frank Melville Jr.
Here was a man whose heart was good,
Who walked with men and understood.
His was a hand that asked no fee
For friendliness or kindness done.
And now that he has journeyed on
His is a fame that never ends,
And leaves behind uncounted friends.

I paused and wrote these words down on a scrap of paper from my pocket. Simple but not simplistic, they seemed to capture a universal truth. Frank Melville Jr.'s life was no doubt a mixture of light and shadow. Yet if he lived anything like the life that this affirming eulogy paints, I suspect that he died a satisfied man—in large part because he was at least as interested in the happiness of others as in his own. I walk by these words from time to time and pause anew to consider them.

The gifts of the garden are for all of us.

🌿 FINDING YOUR OWN HIDDEN GIFTS
Giving to Those Who Need the Most

Giving to others, in even the smallest way, is a wonderful gift. Reaching out to people who are suffering real, daily loss—the homeless, hungry, illiterate, dying—is often both difficult and deeply rewarding. This kind of helping can give you the gift of an identity and a role in life, and deepen your sense of meaning and purpose.

It's easy to begin. Find a needful group for which you have a special affinity—people who are confronting struggles in life that are especially moving to you. No one can tell you what group that is, of course, or what kind of work you will do. It might be serving food once a week for an afternoon at a community kitchen for the homeless; it might be using your spare afternoon to tutor folks who cannot read or write; it might be heading down to the sight center to help folks who are blind with their shopping; it might be coaching basketball at the local gym in a program for kids who would otherwise be out on the streets; it might be helping with a "meals on wheels" program to get decent dinners on the tables of debilitated older adults . . .

It really doesn't matter what the cause is. It is simply important in the journey of life, with all its ups and its downs, to have a special place for some needy group that we adopt as our own, and around which we develop our creative abilities to do good in the world. We may not always find ourselves with the time and energy to serve this constituency, but the potential is always there.

Each of us is capable of flourishing in hard times through drawing on our original nature of self-giving love, no matter how obscured or covered over it might be. We should not assume that such love is first and foremost an emotion—though it is this, to be sure. But it is an emotion that derives from a practical skill in helping a needful group, and it can be practiced like other skills. Focus mindfully and actively on the needs of some group with which you have an affinity, and let the gifts of your giving follow.

- **Think about where your passions lie.** Reaching out to a needful group about which you have a certain passion makes your commitment to helping that much stronger. Do you want to save the environment, other pets like yours, people with the same illness that runs in your family, homeless families, victims of natural disasters . . . ? The alternatives are endless.
- **Think about your own skills.** Do you enjoy working one-on-one with people, or do you have great organizational skills? Are you handy with construction tools, or can you put your bookkeeping or legal expertise to use in the service of a needy nonprofit? Do you have language skills that might help others communicate their needs? Reaching out in the way that best suits you helps keep you on track.
- **Contact groups whose interests you share.** If you think you are alone in your passion for a particular cause, think again. There are countless organizations looking for people who want to help. When you find a group whose work is

meaningful to you, call the volunteer coordinator to discover what sorts of helping opportunities are open.

- **Practice concentric visualizations, from the nearest to the neediest.** Here is an exercise you can do anytime. Close your eyes and visualize yourself giving a generous smile to the person in your life you love most. Now open your eyes. How do you feel? Imagine that person smiling back and laughing with you. Next, close your eyes and visualize yourself giving a generous smile to someone who is just an acquaintance, and feel that same response and laughter. Finally, close your eyes and visualize yourself giving a generous smile to someone who you think is really in need of help, and feel that response and laughter. Then, imagine how you can help that person, and go out and do it.

4

The Gift of Deep Happiness

Are you happy you made the move?" In my first months of settling into Stony Brook, my colleague and friend Dr. Iris Granek would ask me this question regularly. She had a lot to do with recruiting me, so this was a natural question.

My response was always a qualified "Well, what do we mean by happiness?" or "I can't really say until I see how this all works out." It was twenty-two months later that I finally was able to respond to her question with an affirmative "Yes, I have been able to do a lot of good things here for a lot of people, so I am pretty happy."

I had always considered myself a happy guy, all things considered. So this new mood of unrest and uprootedness got my attention big-time. I had to actively remember that real happiness, deep happiness, is not a thing we can chase and catch, but a feeling we can access every moment in the way we practice living each day.

❧ THREE TYPES OF HAPPINESS

The question "What is happiness?" is deceptively simple. I believe that we call three very different states of mind by this term, yet only one of them is the one I would call deep happiness.

Happiness based in power over others is the furthest from the source of real joy—the clenched fist rather than the open hand. For some, "staying in power" is all there is; in pursuit of it they sweep over the freedom and dignity of others like a tsunami, destroying all for nothing. These are the Machiavellian CEOs for whom the end always justifies the means—no matter who or what is destroyed in the process. These are the so-called leaders who can only accept unquestioning followers and deem them to be their minions; these are the abusers, no matter how small their world. Leadership for them is not about serving others, but about being served.

Happiness rooted in desire is the one most people probably think of first: the free pursuit of pleasurable experiences, consuming all we crave. But this brings no real satisfaction. When we get what we thought we wanted, it may make us happy for a brief moment—until we feel we need to replace it with something better. We live in a society ruled by image and consumerism. If we just had a cooler car or the latest video game system or a more perfect nose or a younger and more attractive mate, all our troubles would be solved. Yet, as the twentieth-century Hindu sage J. Krishnamurti warned, "It is no measure of health to be well-adjusted to a profoundly sick society." Many Americans today are becoming exhausted chasing after things, and are looking for something more lasting.

These two false types of happiness are ultimately unsatisfying because we must get them from a person or thing *outside* ourselves. The problem with this "external" form of happiness is that we will always be looking for it, and it will always be just out of reach. We grab it, we hold it for a while, and then it's gone. We are left unsatisfied and searching for more. Surprisingly, even when we actively chase power and desires, deep down inside we seem to know what *really* makes us happy. Although changes in our finances can knock us off our feet, and a sudden influx of cash when you have no way to pay the bills may flood your brain with temporary euphoria, research shows that happiness is not dependent on money, and materialism does not make people happy.[1]

In 1976, researchers studied the attitudes of twelve thousand college freshman and then followed up with them almost twenty years later, when they were thirty-seven. The ones who had primarily materialistic aspirations as freshman were less happy with their lives two decades later when compared with the young people who were not materialistically focused.[2]

So what does make us happy? A *Time* poll gives us a snapshot of the American psyche indicating that the connection between helping others and experiencing happiness is something that most people understand. When asked about the sources of their happiness, 75 percent of Americans in this poll indicated that "contributing to the lives of others" was among the top three things that make them happy, The only items that topped this were "friends and friendships" (76 percent), and "relationship with children" (77 percent), both of which involve social connectedness, giving behavior, and social support. These were the top three. Sixty-two percent indicated that spirituality and religious worship were important for their happiness.[3] This is an encouraging poll because it underscores that, despite all the materialistic, greedy, and hedonic images of American happiness, the real face of America is one that smiles in meaningful friendships and in contributing to others.

This sense of happiness is corroborated by the 2005 Pew Research Center social trends report "Are We Happy Yet?" based on a telephone survey of a nationally representative, randomly selected sample of 3,014 adults.[4] In this poll, 34 percent of Americans said they were "very happy," 50 percent said they were "pretty happy," 15 percent said "not too happy," and 1 percent said "don't know." These numbers have been stable since at least 1972, when this particular question was first asked on the General Social Survey of the National Opinion Research Center.

The Pew report indicates that money matters some, but not much. Fifty percent of respondents with family incomes of $150,000 or greater said they were very happy, and 23 percent of those with family incomes below $20,000 said this. Americans' average per capita income has doubled over the past three decades when adjusted for inflation, but only a third of us are very happy. Married people, it turns out, are happier

(43 percent very happy) than the unmarried (24 percent very happy). As a whole, Americans are slightly less happy now than they were in 1950.

Spirituality, too, plays a role. According to the Pew report, people who attend religious services weekly or more are happier (43 percent very happy) than those who attend monthly or less (31 percent very happy), or seldom or never (26 percent very happy).[5] It is my interpretation that a religious community will usually encourage self-giving attitudes and the love of neighbor, and can therefore be understood as allowing members to discover their truer and happier selves.

Taking these polls together, we can say that we'll probably call ourselves happy if we cultivate our spirituality, take care of our marriage if we have one, spend time with close friends, contribute to the lives of others, and have enough money to free us from stress. And if you are fortunate enough to have lots of money, figure out a good way to give much of it away to help others!

And that brings us to the true, deep happiness we are talking about in this chapter, which bubbles up naturally from inside our hearts and souls. This deep happiness is a by-product of a life that is well lived in concern for others, yet does not ignore the basic needs of the self. It involves a generosity of heart and action cultivated with consistency. We can be surrounded by a thousand people who love, worship, and adore us as fans or minions, but until we ourselves become active sources of generosity and giving and love, we will not be happy.

Deep happiness provides an inward stability that allows us to sustain joy in our lives. Cultivating this became an important aspect of navigating a difficult relocation.

THE FORMULA FOR DEEP HAPPINESS

You would be right in saying that this information was not new to me—I'm supposed to be the expert, after all! Yet I was still experiencing the wash of mixed feelings that naturally arise when we have to make a big move in uncertain times. Happiness can seem very far away.

Our relatively simple Ohio life had suddenly become more complicated. The tempo of New York was certainly fast, elbows seemed bigger and tempers a little shorter, and everything was so expensive. And any new job has its own stresses, especially as the entire state economy goes in the tank.

We all face challenges. The key is how we respond. I applied a formula for happiness that in the previous five years I had worked on as a research project, and that now was the hope for my own soul. It boils down to letting happiness naturally arise from a combination of four elements:[6]

1. Foremost, *love others!* Show an interest in them, be concerned, and let their happiness be as important to you as your own. Like a child at play, you are not directly pursuing your own happiness, but happiness will find you.
2. Cultivate *moral integrity*. Do not become a house divided. Be consistent in the values and virtues that matter to you.

Otherwise you will never feel whole or at peace in your heart and conscience. Virtue really is its own reward.

3. Enjoy *thankful simplicity.* An attitude of gratitude does bring happiness, and staying materially simple allows for gratitude rather than endless accumulation, and it keeps you from being diverted to meaningless goals.

4. *Stay true to your higher purposes.* Stay on course, have good nonmaterial goals in life, and integrate them deeply. Life is a lot happier without the inner turmoil and torment that come from low ideals and the absence of higher purposes.

These four elements of happiness are often connected to a spiritual foundation—if not to an organized religion, then to the belief that our lives on this earth are best lived in relation to some presence in the universe that loves us all in wisdom, constancy, purity, and intensity. Let's take a closer look at how these elements work in real life.

LOVE OTHERS

Long after much of the science around "happiness" fades, one benchmark in the research will stand the test of time: sustainable happiness is primarily the result of contributing to the lives of others. When we become preoccupied with ourselves and our resentments, when we cannot think beyond ourselves, we lose the joy of living. The antidote is to actively reach out and help others in a way that they desire and appreciate. When we give to others without thinking of ourselves, we set free the single most essential element in a happy life. If there is some "secret" to happiness, this is it.

My friend and former student Sara Laskey is now an emergency room doctor in Cleveland, but she studied improvisation and clowning before she decided to pursue a medical career. Now she puts her training to work every day giving patients and their worried families the gift of humor. "For me, making someone laugh is very pleasurable," she says. "You create a connection with somebody. If something happens and you're both laughing, for that second you are in the same place at the same time. So often in life we sort of pass each other; we're just living side by side. So those moments when you can make someone laugh—and I don't care if it's in the circus or around your dinner table—those are things that are very memorable.

"I like to do this same thing with my patients in the emergency department," she explains. "Obviously, not everyone is in a position to be able to laugh, but I'll kind of joke around or make a funny comment sometimes to make a connection with somebody, sometimes to gauge where they are physically. If they can respond with laughter, that gives me a sense of where they are in their pain spectrum and where they are in their immediate recovery, and so often it helps to diffuse situations of high anxiety and calm everybody down."

Sara's story reminds me of this passage from St. Paul: "God loves a cheerful giver" (2 Corinthians 9:7). Love does not allow us to hold on to our miseries, and it must be passed along, or it dissipates like an electrical current. Love is like the sun, and we are like sunflowers. The more we are turned toward love, the more abundantly we live. And this love is the glue that binds us together with others in the communities that make life joyful.

A person who appreciates the power of love in his or her own life will never close the door on receiving from others. My friend Amy is a wonderfully joyful person who runs a preschool in a local church where my family worshiped for many years. She loves every child there, and always seems strikingly happy. When I asked her to tell me how she can be so happy, she said, "My life is filled with the sights, sounds, and spirits of young children. Each day I am given the gift of renewed innocence as I look at the world alongside new spirits who experience life with fresh eyes and mountains of hope. Children call us to a different way of *seeing*. . . . The children I have taught and held and loved have also, in their uniquely child ways, taught and held and loved me. I have learned to trust in a hope so basic and entrenched in my being it was easily covered over with more important 'adult things.'"

This is beautiful to see, and is something that is within reach for each of us. Like Amy and Sara, we can all be teachers and transmitters of love. When we look back on our lives, it is most inspiring to see generous love in the hearts of our friends, our children, our students, and all those for whom we have been models and teachers. We can live passable lives without ever inspiring others to love through our example, but we cannot truly flourish without passing this torch to the world around us.

Today's young people may be turning away from over-concern with career and money, and actively working to better the environment and help those who are in need around the world. Even more impressive, this unselfish outreach holds for some of the wealthiest and most privileged members of society who are no longer satisfied with writing checks and forgetting about it. They want to experience deeper connectivity, high resonance, and integral involvement with projects that make the world a better place. Doctors who could be sitting at home enjoying their high salaries are instead flying to regions in crisis with Doctors Without Borders and other organizations. Bill Gates, the founder of Microsoft, decided to spend his billions not on himself but on his effort to enhance health care around the world. Increasingly, the young founders of highly successful dot-com companies like eBay and Google are building direct philanthropy into their companies, and engaging employees in face-to-face helping to create a new mosaic of meaning in the business world. Actors and actresses head out of town to involve themselves personally in helping activities. My friend Dr. John Shanley, also in the Department of Preventive Medicine at Stony Brook, was down in Haiti after the earthquake with a team of doctors and nurses when he saw actor Harrison Ford seated in a small restaurant. Ford had flown in with his plane mechanic to fly supplies around the island. People derive a great deal of joy from being helpful to others.

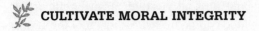 **CULTIVATE MORAL INTEGRITY**

The word *morality* is much overused in our society, and the word *integrity* sadly neglected. Yet without moral integrity—the habit of acting out our deepest ethical and spiritual foundation, following our conscience—we can never experience deep happiness. Every significant and successful spiritual tradition teaches an ethics of integrity, often in the context of the Golden Rule in its benevolent formulation, "Do unto others as you would have them do unto you":

Buddhism: Hurt not others in ways that you yourself would find hurtful. (Udana-Varga 5,18)

Confucianism: Surely it is the maxim of loving-kindness: Do not unto others that you would not have them do unto you. (Analects 15,23)

Islam: No man is a true believer unless he desireth for his brother that which he desireth for himself. (Azizullah-Hadith 150)

Taoism: Regard your neighbor's gains as your own gain and your neighbor's loss as your own loss. (T'ai Shang Kan Ying P'ien)

Zoroastrianism: That nature alone is good which refrains from doing unto another whatsoever is not good for itself. (Dadistan-i-dinik 94–5)

Jain: A man should treat all creatures in the world as he himself would like to be treated. (Wisdom of the Living Religions, no. 69-I:II:33)

Brahmanism: This is the sum of duty: do naught unto others which would cause you pain if done to you. (Mahabharata 5,1517)

The Golden Rule in its positive formulation, "Do unto others," is the greatest self-help formula ever devised. Individual responsibility is central: each of us can be instruments of moral inspiration if we choose to.

When we violate the principles we hold dear, we feel the contradiction immediately. When we violate our own souls, we can become despondent and even depressed. It is impossible to be happy and feel inwardly whole when what we do violates who we feel we are.

Integrity—walking our talk—is a foundation of deep happiness. And people who model integrity in this way send ripples of influence into the world, literally transmitting happiness to others. Perhaps one of the finest examples was the children's television host Mr. Rogers, who I was privileged to call my friend. As an ordained Presbyterian minister, Fred Rogers felt called to be a model of compassion and respect to encourage children from all over the world—or, as he put it, "I went into television because I hated it so, and I thought there was some way of using this fabulous instrument to be of nurture to those who would watch and listen."[7] Mr. Rogers looked through our television screens with the eyes of compassion, saw us just as we are, and loved us for it. His happiness was unquestionable; his glow infused everyone who came in contact with him. He had the glow of integrity.

My friend Larry Marshall, a psychologist, was not famous, but he was one of the most genuinely happy people I have ever known, and he integrated that quality into everything he did, even at the end of his life. His wife, Patty, was a colleague of mine, and always extremely busy at work. She told me that in his last days, his entire focus was on her well-being after his death. So long as he was lucid, he gave her instructions on how to handle the chores that he had so reliably performed for her. Through love, Larry was giving to the end, and in this his dying was noble and as joyous as it could be. Larry did not seem especially anxious about or fearful of death. His happiness was serene. Larry died at age seventy— not an especially long life these days. Yet the fact that he died as he lived—a generous, caring, and happy man—tells us that this serene joy is the greatest fruit of a life lived as much for others as for self. Larry was happy because he had faith that happiness would come along on its own, and it did.

Larry's remembrance service was the most inspiring I have ever attended. St. Ann's Church in Cleveland Heights was packed that morning. Patty spoke joyfully of how Larry brought love into her life and their children's lives; a brother spoke of Larry's companionship over the years; a local friend spoke of him as always willing to take a walk with anyone who needed him; a friend from Chicago spoke of how Larry befriended prisoners who were on death row. The priest, Father Jim, said that Larry had made the world a better place. For the entire hour, the language was consistently about love. Larry loved people, and people loved Larry. Everyone spoke of how Larry kept thinking of the people he loved. Even as he struggled with the pain of an aggressive cancer, he was regularly jotting down helpful ideas for people that would make their lives a little easier when he was gone, including lots of "how to" notes for Patty about maintaining the house, cooking turkey soup, and taking care of the dog. Larry was always a giver who asked what he could do for others rather than what they could do for him, and he was one of the happiest men I have known. I played some classical guitar as my contribution to the service, and left feeling that even in death, Larry somehow brought people together in a way that celebrated his love.

Later, Patty later offered the following words in a memo to me regarding Larry's diagnosis: "On the evening of the day we were told the diagnosis, together we telephoned every one of our brothers and sisters to let them know. After the phone calls were made we talked and talked. We talked about the most important things you can say to someone you love. We talked about our love, about little hurts and apologies, about forgiveness and deep gratitude. It was a conversation about all the essential aspects of living in love, with respect and gratitude, and with forgiveness too—because we are all so very human."

Larry loved widely, acknowledged everyone, dressed fairly simply, had tremendous integrity, and was profoundly reliable. Larry just thought of himself as an everyday guy living a caring life. He always seemed self-possessed, kind, and joyful, even when Patty had herself become seriously ill several years before his death. His warmth and smile were indisputable marks of his underlying satisfaction with his life. He was not seeking a purpose in life, because he had found one.

The most supremely happy people I have known have lived in an emotional energy so warm and palpable that it seems to grow only more intense and expansive over time, and it is the source of happiness. Their love defies the second law of thermodynamics: the more love they give, the more there is to be given.

ENJOY THANKFUL SIMPLICITY

This world is too darn cluttered. There is just so much stuff, and we keep collecting it and consuming it, and it is not making us happier. Surveys show that people living in less materialistic countries are happier than we are, so long as they have enough to get by and plenty of community. And when people accumulate a lot more than enough, what makes them happiest is giving it away in meaningful ways. I see restaurants on every corner and people eating away, but too many of them are deprived of the nourishment they need to be happy. They suffer starvation of a sort, no matter how big the plate before them. Research has shown time and again that if they could take that $20 and spend it on the real needs of another human being, they would be happier. For many, easy money is poison. Every year—in my role as trustee of a philanthropic foundation—I go down to Nassau for a meeting at Paradise

Island, a big hotel and gambling resort. Some James Bond movies have been filmed in the casino there. I spent a whole hour one day looking for the glamour and never finding it. I counted about two hundred people, most of whom looked sad or anxious, standing in front of machines awaiting some fluke of fate, some lucky number that would make them happy in the selfish way of beating the odds. Of the ten people who won while I was watching, not one smiled.

Jean Vanier is a humble man of Catholic faith who is now in his late seventies. He began L'Arche Farm and Gardens in 1964, and has devoted his life to honoring the humanity of persons with cognitive disabilities.[8] He has said,

> Soon after L'Arche began, I came across the passage in Luke's gospel in which Jesus says: "When you give a luncheon or a dinner, do not invite your friends or your brothers. But when you give a banquet, invite the poor, the crippled and you will be blessed" (Luke 14: 12–14). I had heard this text often, but its full force had never struck me. Suddenly, I realized that it described what we were living at L'Arche. . . . It was a way of life absolutely opposed to the values of a competitive, hierarchical society in which the weak are pushed aside.[9]

Jean stays close to the simple delights of the farm, where I joined him in 2008 for a week just to get a feel for his simple environs. And each day he devotes himself to the love of others in such a way that he too is much beloved. He is a happy man in the deepest sense of the word. Through his organization, he has passed the torch of this joy-through-love to tens of thousands of young assistants. Not long ago I was invited to write a letter to the Nobel Peace Prize Committee on his behalf, and I hope someday he wins it.

Our possessions can do wonderful things—connect us with others, make life just a little easier, show us the world. But our fascination with them has the power to divert our attention from our real beauty: our natural capacity to reach out to others in love. More than a thousand years ago, the Roman philosopher Marcus Aurelius wrote, "Remember that very little is needed to make a happy life." And he had it exactly right.

Thankful simplicity allows us to find delight in the beauty of life that is available to us all—the waves of the ocean along the shore, a cool breeze on a summer afternoon, the warm glow of an outdoor fire, a quiet moment of companionship. The simple gifts of life are infinitely wondrous when we take a moment to stop and look around us. Clouds and sun, the red and gold of autumn leaves, ice and snow, shells and streams, trees in spring, fireside conversation, meals eaten together, games in the open air, the satisfaction of a lute suite well played in the evening, the simple dedication to learning and truth—all things plain yet elegant. Simplicity allows us to celebrate nature, to be attuned to the generative planet Earth on which we live.

One of the very core spiritual emotions is awe or wonder. I worry that these days, with our heads buried in text messaging and e-mail, we are missing out on that. I find awe in natural beauty, music, and art and poetry as most of us do. But sometimes it seems that people's lives are so focused on more and more things in higher and higher piles that they cannot see the God-given beauty of the generative earth around them or in a smile or in a simple act of kindness. We need to be a little more mystical about nature and see its beauties as a window into the divine source. What an amazingly colorful and wondrous planet we live on.

🌿 STAY TRUE TO YOUR HIGHER PURPOSE

Through the turmoil of our relocation, I was sustained by the sense that what I was building at Stony Brook was meaningful. I threw myself into the work I had been hired to perform: developing the Center for Medical Humanities, Compassionate Care, and Bioethics, located in the School of Medicine in the Department of Preventive Medicine.

Compassion—always moving past the sense that one is the center of the universe and responding wisely to suffering when one sees it—is the heart of love and giving, and the wellspring of deep happiness. Working with compassion in the hospital setting may seem obvious; but if you ask patients about their experiences in clinical settings, too many say they felt overly objectified: "To the doctors, I was just the kidney in room 5." In Ohio I saw a doctor barge into a hospital room without even knocking. The patient, a middle-aged woman, was lying naked on the bed. A dozen medical students followed right in. The patient began to shake and cry she was so upset. The doctor was at the end of a busy day and operating on less than five hours of sleep; the students were similarly stressed. But deep down, they all understood that there was no real excuse for their behavior.

It would have been possible for the doctor to have knocked on the door and asked, "Would you be okay if I came in with some medical students? Do you need a few minutes to get ready? Thanks so much." Medical students are demoralized and disenchanted when they experience a clinical environment that is dehumanizing and uncaring. The bottom line is that the medical students know bad role modeling when they see it, and we work to inoculate them against such things through discussion groups and encouragement. The poor overworked residents (newly graduated medical students who gain valuable experience in caring for patients in residency programs in hospitals before they become licensed in their specialties) suffer as well from the lack of compassionate care. Sleep-deprived residents just don't have the energy left for compassionate care unless they are really mindful of its value. They are lucky if they can muster enough energy to get home and grab a bite to eat. They often do go through a period when they feel taken advantage of by patients, and become less trusting and naïve; but they can bounce back from this valley pretty quickly.

Possibly the most often quoted words in American medical history are those of Dr. Francis W. Peabody, delivered to the Harvard Medical School class in 1925: "One of the essential qualities of the clinician is interest in humanity, for the secret of the care of the patient is in caring for the patient."[10]

Without caregivers who demonstrate this basic caring attitude and emotion, patients experience an exquisite isolation that is a significant risk factor for morbidity and mortality comparable to obesity, sedentary lifestyle, and smoking. Pastoral care heals, good nurses and social workers do too, but good doctors also have to make the connections that patients need.

So our work in the Center is not just with medical students but with residents, seasoned clinicians, staff, and the entire health care system. People are desperate for this work. Martin Luther King Jr., Mother Teresa, and many others have written that the real fields for missionary activity in the world today are in affluent countries where people have succumbed to consumerism and emptiness, and have lost their idealism with regard to their professional lives. These are good people, but they need deep transformation, and they need to be refreshed. This sense of mission certainly sustained me through the early years at Stony Brook.

Meaningful work is a blessing, and it is critical to resilience. As the late mythologist Joseph Campbell famously said, "Follow your bliss." Over the years, I have seen so many people miss their calling and end up doing something they did not love, mostly for the money. They took a job that may have paid a little more, but that had nothing to do with who they were as people. They just could not be passionate about their work; they could not honestly say that at the deepest level, they really wanted to be responsible for the things they had to do; they were going through the motions, living on dry duty, and not fully engaged; they were trying to give something to the world that they never really possessed in the first place. And as a result, they were running on empty, feeling alienated from their true calling.

Still, we are sometimes forced into jobs that help us pay the bills and support our loved ones, and there is no blame or shame in that. But it is crucial to be able to identify these jobs as occupations (*occupare*) that "occupy" time and pay the bills. Or we may have a career (*careo*) that "carries" us forward to retirement. But without a calling (*vocacio*) that involves us fully, our happiness is generally not as great as it could be. If we are very fortunate, our true calling will also be the way we earn a living. But even if this happy intersection does not occur, it is still possible to search out and act on our special gifts, no matter our age or circumstance. It is never too late to experience deep happiness.

HAPPINESS IN THE MIDST OF SADNESS

Please do not come away from this chapter thinking that you should be perfectly happy 100 percent of the time. That is simply not possible. Sadness is bound up with happiness, part of the rich emotional texture of life; and inevitably, we experience both happiness and sadness. Life is like a beautiful piece of music—there have to be contrasts between sound and silence, high and low, fast and slow, soft and loud. In these contrasts a piece of music becomes interesting. Similarly, they make our lives interesting. The key is to come away from our suffering with increased determination to experience the inevitable sadness as a wave on the ocean of a deeper happiness.

As I write these words almost two years after moving to Long Island, I can truly say that we are feeling comfortable here. Speaking only for myself, it took a full year for me to get past the unexpected grief over leaving Cleveland, which over twenty years had become a part of me. And this really did take me by surprise. I am an upbeat guy who likes to create happiness where it doesn't exist. Even in cloud-covered places like Portland or Cleveland, the absence of the sun never makes me depressed at all, and depression is something that to date I have never had to confront; I guess my genetic "set point" on happiness is pretty high. Still, the extent of my adjustment over leaving caught me unawares. I had to learn that sadness and happiness can coexist.

Numerous astonishing people do suffer from depression. Abraham Lincoln has been described quite vividly as suffering from depression throughout his life. One biographer wrote of a depressive episode in 1840–1841, when Lincoln came close to killing himself: "As a young man, he stepped back from the brink of suicide, deciding he must live to do some meaningful work."[11] He "self-medicated" by engaging in storytelling and humor, giving to others through a mirth that equally elevated his own spirits. He found comfort in jokes and stories, in a desire to do something in his life that would "redound to the interest of his fellow man," in a deep empathy for the suffering of others, and in divine providence.

Lincoln helped others whenever he could, even in as simple an act as going into the train station in Washington, D.C., and offering to help a young girl lift up her large suitcase. As he put it, "When I do good, I feel good; when I do bad, I feel bad." Lincoln was the helper therapy principle in action against gloom.

Some degree of sadness is just the stuff of life. I find it troubling that people feel they must have a relentless smile. If we don't feel happy every moment of every day, we need to wait it out, compensating with self-giving love, generous acts, moral integrity, gratitude, nonmaterial values, and a sense that God will see us through over time. One day, when I was feeling all the stresses of learning a new work environment, new personalities, and new politics at the university, and of dealing with some domestic and financial challenges, I jumped on the ferry with my laptop and began writing— letters to old friends, and part of this book. In writing I found solace and peace, and my joy returned.

I really *like* the Center, and am so grateful that I had the chance to hire great people and teach such wonderful medical students—perhaps the best I have ever encountered in almost thirty years of such teaching. I have a lot of happiness in my life here, and much has been gained.

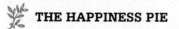 **THE HAPPINESS PIE**

According to the scientific researchers—and everyday life experience!—much of our happiness is up to us as individuals— regardless of the predispositions we are born with, and regardless of circumstances, however challenging. Researchers estimate the percentages differently, but I like to divide the happiness pie into three pieces that are bound to vary in size according to the individual.

One piece is biology.[12] Just as some people are hardwired to be skinny and others seem to gain weight just by looking at food, some people are naturally happier than others. Yet I believe, with Abraham Lincoln, that "a man is about as happy as he makes up his mind to be." Yes, some babies are born smiling and content, and others are born kicking and crying. But whatever hand we are dealt, we choose how to play the cards.

Another piece of the happiness pie is influenced by external circumstances—an uplifting environment, proximity to nature, good parents and a loving family, available nonparent mentors, a chance at a good education, and a satisfying job. Living in a downtrodden neighborhood, having to worry a lot about how to scrape by without going into foreclosure in your house, getting fired from a job you love because the economy tanked—these things really do make it harder to be happy.[13]

The final piece of the happiness pie—regardless of our genetic predisposition or life circumstances—is how we choose to play the cards we've been dealt. Our own behavior, attitudes, activities, practices, and responses ultimately determine our happiness.

Yes, genetic predisposition and circumstances matter. But we human beings are free creatures, and we can rise above it all in resilience, in post-traumatic growth, in an impassioned hope that makes impossibilities real. When we touch infinite love in prayer or meditation, or feel the exuberance of creative self-giving love, our old limits fall away, and we leap above the crazy seas of sorrow into the light and touch the sky.

My friend Larry was such a striking model of deep happiness in ordinary life that he might seem unusual—special. But he would have been the first to say that he was not special. Nor is it necessary to be naturally happy to be a vehicle for deep happiness. Be like a child at play—follow your bliss and have faith that happiness will find you.

🌿 FINDING YOUR OWN HIDDEN GIFTS
Deep Happiness

Even Abraham Lincoln, who today might be diagnosed as clinically depressed, found a route out of the darkness. That route is available to all of us. Remember, happiness pursued eludes—my friend Sir John Templeton, who died in 2008, said this many times. He liked the Declaration of Independence, which gives us the inalienable right to the "pursuit of happiness," but he pointed out that the pursuit of happiness is never successful, because the more you pursue it selfishly, the less it will be achieved. Happiness for Sir John was never an end in itself, but a by-product: a hidden gift of helping others.

- **Get the "helping-happiness loop" started.** We know that happier people do tend to be more giving and helpful than unhappy people. But we also know, from more than ten intervention studies, that people who are unhappy and help others report feeling greater happiness. This forms a classic feedback loop. When we are feeling unhappy, it can be hard to take action. So right now, tell yourself that the next time you feel unhappy you will find someone in a needy situation and help him or her out—anything from helping a child tie her shoe, getting a can off the top shelf in the grocery store for a person who can't quite reach it, giving a dollar to a homeless person . . . anything. Check in with yourself: Are you feeling even a *little* better? Then repeat this exercise. Helping increases happiness, which increases helping, which increases happiness.

- **Practice gratitude.** Get in the habit of giving thanks for something every day. Make a point of giving thanks in the morning on the way to school or work, just before eating that first bite of lunch, before an evening meal . . . the time you choose is up to you. Just think thankfully of one or two things that come to mind. You can do this as a short prayer, as a little thought exercise, by making a list or keeping a journal—whatever comes naturally. When we are thankful, we cannot be unhappy. This may sound naïve, but it is a proven fact.

- **Aim for true friendships.** Friends aren't just people we party with. A real friend is the one person who cares about your moral integrity and will let you know that your behavior is off track and inconsistent with your dreams. If you do not already have such a relationship, prime the pump. Choose someone you trust—a pastor, a mentor, or an acquaintance you suspect has the makings of a good friend—and ask that person if you can tell him or her something in confidence that you need help with. Then honestly tell this person about something you said or did that wasn't noble, that wasn't you at your best, and ask that person to bring this subject up with you once a month, just to keep you on track. After a while, ask your friend if there is some behavior in his or her life that he or she wants to mention and that you can check up on every month. This kind of friendship is exactly what Aristotle meant by the third and highest form of *philia*, friendship.

- **Create a helping-happiness network.** Just as there is a helping-happiness loop that operates in the individual, there is a contagious sort of helping-happiness loop that operates through networks of people. We all have the capacity to be helpful to needy people. Once you identify an individual or a group that you feel called to help in a special way, get involved right away. As soon as possible, invite your friends to come along with you and be part of a little network of helping. Most people who really make a big difference in the world through caring are just ordinary folks like you and me, but they have a passion for something that ignites a happiness around helping that they can pass on to everyone with whom they come in contact.

- **Find your own kindness = happiness dose.** Positive psychologist Sonja Lyubomirsky has shown that research subjects who perform acts of kindness (five acts on a single day each week) tend to feel happier after six weeks.[14] An act of kindness can be as small as picking up a worm from the sidewalk after a rain and placing it gently back in the dirt. I would suggest also trying one act a day, each and every day, as did the author of 29 *Gifts*, as she was struggling with her multiple sclerosis.[15] Different strokes for different folks—one size does not fit all. Experiment and find the right dose and intensity of helping to make *you* happy.

5

The Gift of Compassion and Unlimited Love

I am no flashy mystic with some marketable new vision—just a simple mainstream Christian trying in a small way to contribute to the practice and knowledge of self-giving love in a culture and a world that often seem to run in the opposite direction. But like a majority of Americans, I have intuited an ultimate reality of love. And I had one surprising experience of union with what I can only call pure love: beyond time, expansive, luminous, unlimited in the sense of being fully accepting.

One early Sunday morning, at age twenty-three, I sat down after waking up at about five to meditate and pray a bit. Immediately afterward, as I was nodding off, I felt suddenly overwhelmed by a powerful tingling sensation over my whole body. I felt incredible warmth and had the sense of leaving time and space behind. I felt surrounded by very bright light and by a warm love that was beyond anything I had ever known or deserved. For about ten or fifteen minutes, I felt as though I were in another world, with another form of consciousness.

117

It was at first quite scary, but then I felt deeply connected with an ultimate love, enveloped in God's presence, and it was at once both deeply peaceful and free of myself. This was all ineffable, and though words fail, I will never forget these moments. At the time I was living in a brown row house on 45th street in Philadelphia, not far from the University of Pennsylvania, and I can remember the details of that room and morning as vividly as anything in my life. It made a real impression.

This event was not the result of intellect or of knowledge, or of any action on my part. It was pure gift or grace. Yet for me, at that moment, it was perfectly confirming—we are all accepted in God's surprisingly deep love regardless of the mixed-up feelings, thoughts, and actions that at times drag down our lives. I suppose that was how this experience made me feel: fully accepted and in God's hands. This love felt close or intimate in the same sense that one would feel this from a good parent, a good friend, or a good sibling. There was a sense of special personal connection, of being cherished. Love, in order to be love, must have a personal element, affirming the significance of an individual in all his or her particularity.

These days, thoughtful people have to be ambivalent about "God" because depending on how believers conceive of God, their belief can bring out the very best or the very worst in them. So why not start referring to God as Unlimited Love, being explicit about the divine nature? This would preclude people from ever thinking of God as Unlimited Hatred or Unlimited Anger, and it might help bring out the very best more consistently. I write this as I am about to leave to speak to a philanthropic audience about friend Jean Vanier, whose lifelong work building L'Arche is clearly an example of what taking God-as-Love seriously can mean to the world. If we continue to think of God as something other than Unlimited Love, we will remain a species on the brink of self-annihilation.

MY JOURNEY TOWARD UNLIMITED LOVE

As an adolescent at school in New Hampshire, I read a lot of the mystics. Except for sacred studies and math, which I considered related, I wasn't that interested in academics. I did love classical and blues guitar, and running long distances in the hilly woods around Concord.

In my teens, I met Rev. Gary Davis, the renowned blind African American folk guitarist who was a big part of the folk revival movement of the 1960s. Davis, who then lived in Jamaica, Queens, was one of the most famous blues and gospel guitarists of his generation, with a career that started in Durham, North Carolina, in the 1930s. He later became an ordained Baptist minister. In the summers I would sit in his steamy apartment in Queens and play "Negro spirituals" and ragtime. Davis, always wearing thick dark sunglasses, would listen to me, occasionally injecting a suggestion or playing along. He thought *agape* love was the single most important thing in the universe. Music was how he spread the Gospel, and we talked as much about God's love as we ever did about blues or ragtime. One day, as we were playing "Amazing Grace," Davis interrupted me abruptly as though he were inspired suddenly from above: "Stevie, you play pretty good, but you got to actually *study love*. That is what I feel." Davis either really intuited a calling for me or was nicely saying that life as a professional guitarist was not in the cards.

This relationship encouraged me to do an independent study project on the theology of love with Rev. Rodney Welles, who is still actively working with the homeless in Wilmington, Delaware. I read everything I could of the writings of such African Americans as Howard Thurman, Benjamin Elijah Mays, and Martin Luther King Jr., all of the Morehouse College world in Atlanta. It was the love-mystic Thurman who first visited Gandhi in India in the mid-1930s and brought him to the attention of Mays and eventually King. I still keep their books within reach.

They taught that love in our culture had to be redescribed as a public concept, rather than as something limited to the confines of the nuclear family or to the chatter of romantic infatuation. They asserted a broad and less restrained con-cept of love as a public and political concept. This is a love as understood historically in the Abrahamic traditions, in Hinduism and Buddhism, and beyond. In these great spiritual traditions, love does not end in the confines of marriage, friendship, and family. Rather, love is the foundation of a new society, a Beloved Community, as King would write, quoting the Harvard philosopher of love, Josiah Royce, or the sociolo-gist Sorokin. I was struck by the connection these great men made between love and flourishing. They did not think that a life of deep love was one of self-flagellation and unhappiness.

Rather, they connected this broad love with hope, faith, and joy. They were buoyant, cheerful, and effervescent people. I was sometimes tutored in this by Rev. John T. Walker, who taught at St. Paul's School before going off to become the dean of the National Cathedral in Washington, D.C., though he returned regularly to preach on love and justice.

In the summer of 1969, I hitched across the country on Route 80, and for a while I lived out in San Francisco's Mission District with my cousin George, who was then an apartment superintendent. George was a bright guy with a degree from the University of North Carolina at Chapel Hill, but heavy combat in Vietnam had left him adrift in life. He drove a motorcycle and was part of the Vietnam vet subculture. I joined a Buddhist storefront temple, regularly chanting and spending time with some interesting folks, mostly Japanese Americans. This was a Nichiren Buddhist community, known for its techniques of chanting the words *nam myoho renge kyo*, and they talked a lot about compassion as their core spiritual value. An older man named Gus caringly became my mentor, and he insisted that I adhere to a strict path. He often said that "drugs make a mockery of the soul," and this stayed with me. With old Gus sometimes accompanying me, I spent the rest of the summer playing classical guitar in Hispanic restaurants, reading a lot of Buddhist writings, doing love meditations in the storefront, and reading some Christian thinkers as well.

In September I hitched over the Golden Gate Bridge and up the Pacific Coast Highway for my freshman year at Reed College in Oregon, which had given me a scholarship.

It is a school for somewhat unusual people. At that time, if a young person truly was a seeker and did not really want to be in college, Reed was the place to go. It was expected that half the students would drop out after a year or so, and they tended to. I arrived in the early evening to the sound of loud music and a psychedelic light show in progress, projected on an inflated white plastic tent perched on the front lawn. I saw a balding man with curly red hair, holding a can of beer in one hand and a marijuana joint the size of a cigar in the other. I asked him, "Sir, is this Reed College?" He smiled, revealing an American flag embedded in his upper-right front tooth. "Yeah, little buddy," he answered, exhaling in my face. As he wandered away, I asked a kid my own age who that man was. "Ken Kesey," he replied. Kesey was up in Oregon writing his second novel, *Sometimes a Great Notion*, and this was his one day to visit the Reed campus.

That night, I called my mom back east and told her I had made it to college and that the very first person I met was Ken Kesey. She was silent for about a full minute, and I knew she was anxious—she'd read *The Electric Kool-Aid Acid Test*, Tom Wolfe's account of Kesey and his merry band of psychedelic pranksters. "Mom," I said quickly, "don't worry about a thing. He had no influence on me whatsoever!"

In fact, he didn't, and I count myself lucky. In this summer of 1969, it seemed as though an entire generation and more broke away from restricting conventions in the name of "free love." Ironically, in the chaos of this freedom in the name of love, so much of the wisdom and loyalty of love was lost. As Gus said, a lot of folks made a mockery of their souls. In many ways, the guidance I received from my good fortune of meeting people like Rev. Gary Davis and Gus saved me from a lot of suffering. They were spiritual mentors, people who passed the torch across generations, and without them I might have wandered down a very different path.

After a few semesters at Reed, I myself contributed to the already high college attrition rate and became a California quester, dropping in on lots of spiritual groups, eastern and western, old and new, and reading everything I could in world religions. After about a year, I decided to go back to New York to play music and find another college to avoid the draft. My first job after school was in New York City. I lived on 73rd Street and York Avenue in an old five-story walk-up owned by Cornell Medical School, where I was employed as a research assistant in pediatric endocrinology (hormones). I began playing classical guitar concerts around town, mostly in old churches or libraries, which got me back to reading a lot of Christian theology and listening to public lectures by theologians around Manhattan seminaries.

Eventually, I sorted out questions of faith and embraced the basic Christianity of my youth, but at a much deeper level—so much so that I felt that it was time to study *agape* love more formally. After a couple of years working in immunology in Philadelphia, I headed off to do a Ph.D. at the University of Chicago Divinity School. I wrote a dissertation on reconciling self-giving love with deeper happiness, just the same kind of topic that I had worked on at St. Paul's as a kid. I was poised and ready to embark on what would be my life's work. But in fact it would be many years—not until 2001, to be exact—before Sir John Templeton asked me to join him at the Institute of Unlimited Love.[1]

Sir John's idea was wonderful: to fund excellent science through competitive requests for proposals to study how it is that love goes beyond the ordinary limits to include all humanity without exception, and how spirituality fits into this expansion. In 2002, our first proposals yielded 320 letters of intent from researchers around the country, from which we eventually funded twenty studies.

Sir John was not pessimistic about human nature; but he did not have great confidence in the frailties of human love alone, unenlivened by something more. He tended not to speak so much of God as of Unlimited Love. In fact, Unlimited Love was God by a new and clearer name. Sir John believed that Unlimited Love is God's essence and might even be shown to underlie the very energy of the universe. Such love is different in kind from human love because it is different in source. This love seeks no payback, and brings joy to those who experience it. Of course, millions of others in a wide range of spiritual traditions would generally agree with him, and this makes Unlimited Love epistemologically plausible in the sense that if someone viewed all of humanity from space, he or she would be astounded by the number of people across the globe who engage in worship of a loving God.

🌿 SCIENTIFIC PERSPECTIVES ON LOVE

We can't study Unlimited Love directly, as if it were a measurable force, but we can study people's self-reported experience of it and see whether their lives are inspired to love in an enduring and powerful way. Research into Unlimited Love allows that there may be some form of perfectly unconditional, pure, enduring, wise, effective, and all-inclusive love—whether you call it "God's love" or "Godly love" or some other name. This love regards each of us equally, no one more than anyone else. That in itself is profoundly significant.

Our institute has been able to fund more than eighty scientific studies at premier research universities. One of the primary things we have shown is that love of others and love of self are not in any essential opposition unless the self-expenditure of the giving self becomes so demanding that it undermines the care of the self. The reason people assume that self-giving love and self-love are opposed is that they think of themselves as independent creatures connected only on the basis of choice. But the truth is that humans are relational and interdependent creatures, and the good of the giver is very often inseparable from that of the recipient. The very use of our capacity to give is part of our flourishing, just as is the use of our eyes, our ears, and our minds.

The commonly held dichotomy of altruism and egoism is based on a false view of being human: it assumes that these two are not at some deeper level one, at least within certain limits.

True, there will be times in life when loving others requires such significant sacrifice of one's personal goals that careful balances must be struck. There are boundaries to be clarified in order that one not become overwhelmed by another. There is much wisdom in the Buddhist idea of "the middle way" on a spectrum between concern for self and for another, and in the Christian idea of an "order of love" that includes the prudential care of the self even as we do "unto others." Our limits are real; sometimes we must relinquish the activities of love of neighbor to others, and seek rest and replenishment. Remember, the corollary of loving our neighbor as ourselves is to love ourselves as we do our neighbor! But limits affirmed, still, when we forget the fundamental oneness and interdependence of our lives in giving and in receiving support, we will not thrive.

Research has shown that in general, people who report significant levels of generous activities live happier, healthier, and longer lives. But there are always exceptions. Bad things happen to all people, no matter how good they are. But on the whole, it's good to be good.

We have learned that loving, altruistic prayers and meditations are good for the person doing them. Altruistic or loving prayer and meditation engages a whole set of neurological and hormonal networks, underscoring the old adage "Practice makes perfect." Just as violinists who play and practice every day have been shown to undergo neurological changes related to the use of their fingers, prayerful visualization of generous actions can actually be reflected in neurological remapping through neuroplasticity and changed "cortical semantic memory." These spiritual practices are ways of enhancing our attentiveness to the things in our lives that remain meaningful, and they can even contribute to the growth of new neurons in the hippocampus, the part of the brain associated with emotion and memory. So the interior life affects our thought process, our emotions, and our dispositions to act in the world in caring ways.

We have learned from items included in the General Social Survey of the National Opinion Research Center/ University of Chicago that half of people in the United States feel a selfless caring for all others on a regular basis, and many feel this daily.[2]

Sir John had in mind a warm, unselfish love that is not held hostage to reciprocal calculations, that extends to a shared humanity, and that raises every possible question about human nature and ultimate reality, including the nature of God. This is the kind of love that is found in the great spiritual traditions, that gets people down to New Orleans after Katrina, that makes otherwise competent medical students real healers, that enlivens the pursuit of justice, and that is fundamental to human development, happiness, and health.

A NATIONAL SURVEY OF UNLIMITED LOVE

Is it "normal" to have faith in a God of Unlimited Love? Or am I part of a fringe group? I know that for many people, this sort of spiritual intuition is a bit more than they can take. Well, beginning in 2008, along with my sociologist colleagues John Green, Margaret Poloma, Matt Lee, we developed a randomized national survey of adults to find out![3]

John Green is considered one of the foremost religion-spirituality survey specialists in the United States today; he is a senior research fellow with the Pew Charitable Trust and has become the go-to scholar for the media when it comes to religion surveys. The survey was conducted nationally by landline telephone in fall 2009, and 1,208 people, randomly selected from all regions of the United States, responded to a fifteen-minute questionnaire. The survey was quite extensive, but the *divine love scale* at the very core of the survey consisted of four items in a battery, all with the same possible responses: "Never or not asked" (the latter because the respondent said he or she does not believe in God), "Once in a while," "Some days," "Most days," "Every day," or "More than once a day." The statements were as follows:

1. Feel God's love as the greatest power in the universe
2. Feel God's love for you directly
3. Feel God's love for you through others
4. Feel God's love increasing your compassion for others

These items were developed by a team of twenty national experts in survey research and spirituality from ten different universities of distinction, and with consultants ranging from Harvey Cox to Lynn G. Underwood, who deserves our acknowledgment on two key questions. The results of these measures show that beneath the surface of American secularism, materialism, and rejection of organized religion there is a depth of experience of God's love.

Specifically, 45 percent of Americans feel God's love at least once a day, and 83 percent have this experience at least "once in a while"; 83 percent of Americans acknowledged that they "felt God's love increasing their compassion for others," and 53 percent claim this experience "on most days" or more frequently. This is a remarkable set of findings that establishes a new standard in survey methods and provides a ready response for those who feel that belief in Unlimited Love is an aberrant behavior![4]

This is worth repeating. In a random survey, 83 percent of Americans say that they feel God's love directly at least "once in a while," and about half feel this with regularity. Fully 83 percent of American adults feel that God's love increases their compassion for others at least occasionally. And the figures show that the experience of God's love and a self-reported increase in compassion for others are very highly correlated.[5]

William James described this correlation in his 1902 classic, *The Varieties of Religious Experience*. Now, more than a century later, we have demonstrated that such self-reports of an enlivened love for others through such experiences of Godly love are normative. This indicates that people feel strongly that a great deal of the goodness in their lives is ultimately a gift from above. We are taken up into a love that is higher than our own, in a kind of grace or indwelling experience that has real impact on our actions.

So the bottom line is that feelings of God's love that quicken one's sense of compassion are extremely high in America.[6] We need to take this seriously as a major dynamic in American spiritual life. Okay, I know this dynamic may not rise to the surface in a two-hour traffic delay on Route 80 while you're trying to get over the George Washington Bridge on a Sunday afternoon. Things get a little edgy, and folks are under a lot of stress. Nevertheless, most people still have the intuition that a Godly love is alive, not dead, and is a transforming part of their lives. So I am like most folks in this. In the academic world, which tends to be so secular, one can feel out of place.

PRACTICE BENEVOLENCE, NOT VIOLENCE

Our survey shows that at least one very strong element in American religious life is the experience of God's love, and the sense that this quickens or enlivens benevolence. In today's uncertain world, this aspect of religious life is crucial.

When religions have put doctrine and force above love, they have created a history of massive evil from torture to terror, from coercion to conflict, from the Inquisition to Al Qaeda. Religious wars are manifestations of a human tribalism and arrogance that brings out the worst in us. When we become so caught up in following every little detail of a religious law—no matter the religion—we begin to worship the religion rather than the God of love who stands behind that religion. And when we forget that God is love, and arrogance creeps in, we get hatred.

Hatred, hostility, and revenge are strong emotions that can engulf our deeper sense of Unlimited Love like a tidal wave. Our experiences of God's love can be distorted by the human filters of groupishness and exclusion, and translate into a willingness to condemn those who happen to see the world differently than we do. We must be on guard to prevent the love of power from overwhelming the power of love.

One of the most difficult injunctions for any of us to follow is to "love our enemies." Far too many kill in God's name under the assumption that they alone know the unfolding purposes of God. Yet it is only by allowing Unlimited Love to bring us a profound love of our ancient enemies that we can expect to avoid increasing destruction. The world shows no signs of becoming greatly less religious; we humans will always have a passion for an ultimate truth that provides a safe haven of emotional security. To the extent that Unlimited Love can be captured in the ritual worlds that religions create, and expressed in such spiritual emotions as forgiveness and compassion, we will have a human future. To the degree that religions fall short of universal divine love, violence will overcome us all. Unlimited Love alone can rightly align the world in harmony and peace, although it must do so through imperfect human agents like ourselves.

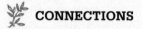
CONNECTIONS

I recommend that people avoid what the Catholic philosopher Jacques Maritain called "angelism," the tendency to think of oneself as an angel. Angels are ethereal; we are real. We live in a human order; we are not winged blithe spirits sweeping across the heavens. We are closer to the earth, dust to dust. Our embodied life lies in places of comfort and common experience, in relationships, in connection.

In mid-February 2010, while our son was on a short trip with a friend's family, Mitsuko and I took a few days off and drove back to Cleveland. We shopped at our favorite stores, visited our old haunts, rejoiced in the company of old friends. On the way back, we stopped at a restaurant, and I picked up a paper that listed the ten cities in the United States where people are unhappiest: Cleveland was number one on the list. We had to laugh—for us, that snowy, rainy, cold, besieged city was still home, the place where our human connections were still alive and well. In fact, Cleveland gets a really bum rap—people there need to fight a lot harder to get the word out on what a good community they have.

The quality of one's life depends on the quality of one's relatedness to others. There is no such thing as a good person in the abstract, but only a good friend, a good neighbor, a good colleague, a good parent, a good spouse, a good citizen. And we are these things in the local school, the local block, the local library, the local neighborhood club. Virtue is not a cloistered thing for humans, however much that may be so for angels. And unlike the angels, who Aquinas taught have knowledge bestowed upon them directly from God, we humans must learn from experience.

When we made this move in mid-2008, I was a bit resentful because loyalty matters a lot to me, and I had not experienced much of it, considering my twenty years of excellent service to an institution. But quickly I realized that my resentment was distancing me from the ways and power of love. Resentment and self-giving simply do not mix. Creativity, hope, gratitude, joy, and just about every human asset wither under the pressure of resentment and bitterness. This was a spiritual turning point, a fork in the road between the light and the shadow. It turned out that the people at Stony Brook were so good that I never had time to get caught up in a lot of destructive emotions. In addition, the people of Cleveland who knew and appreciated me were as loyal as ever and stayed in close touch. I had a wonderful binder full of letters and e-mails wishing me luck and expressing sorrow at my leaving. Prayerful self-giving to build a new world quickly where I had landed was key, and that took, for me anyway, a belief that love rather than hate is the ultimate reality in this universe.

Let me add one thing about our national survey and Unlimited Love. Before the scientific revolution and the Age of Enlightenment, people in the West assumed that the universe was a spiritual place filled with energies and powers and levels of reality that are beyond our full understanding. Whatever the laws of science and the limits of explanation, the majority of people in America still believe that Unlimited Love exists. A majority feel that they have experienced it directly, as well as its working through other people, and they feel that it enlivens their love of others. These are findings that some would prefer not to discuss because it is hard to consider them intellectually. Yet such experiences seem to happen, and to happen often.

The ultimate challenge for the field of science and religion is to figure out if there really are fruits of the spirit, gifts from above, that make kindness, love, forgiveness, gratitude, and joy more than mere human attributes, but things lifted up to higher magnitudes of being and activity through a Higher Power, however understood. Maybe one day someone will actually prove that there is an underlying reality that holds the universe together in love. There may yet come a day when people speak not so much of "God-talk" but of Unlimited Love, knowing that God is love and that love is God.

GOD-WINKS AND GRACE NOTES

Although the universe often seems random and meaningless, we always need to remember that life is a gift from God and that there is meaning and purpose behind it. One way we can remember that is through what I call "God-winks and grace notes"—those improbable yet perfect events in life that some call "just coincidence," but that feel as if they could only be orchestrated from above. Many people want or need to feel that God is working in their lives, and particularly in times of some brokenness; that God's love is absolute despite all their shortcomings; that God has been working in their lives from the very beginning and all along the way to bring them closer. These God-winks are reassuring.

One of the ironies of our move from Cleveland to Setauket was that although Mitsuko and I figured we would weather the storm fairly easily, we were terribly worried about how Andrew would adjust. What a harsh thing to move a youngster away from his lifelong friends! I didn't know it then, but our worry was quite unfounded. This move would turn out to be a tremendous and positive growth experience for our son. Still, at the time, I was dearly in need of a God-wink or two. And, as so often happens, I had to wait for them.

A year-and-a-half after the move, I happened to be in New York City on business and stopped by the Church of St. Thomas on 53rd and Fifth because it is just so beautiful architecturally, and because my dad went there when he was a boy growing up on the upper east side of Manhattan. I stumbled into a noon communion service. After it was over, I approached the priest, Rev. Andrew Mead, and began to tell him about our move and our worries about our son. "Fourteen now," he winced, "that's a tough age."

He told me that when he was that age, his family moved away from a place he liked a lot because his father had to take a new job. He remembered his mother's words exactly: "Andrew, I know this hurts, but we have to do this for Dad." He said that even today, fifty years later, the fact that he recalls such detail shows what a dramatic transition this was. Two

Andrews moving hard at the same age! This was more than coincidence. It was maybe God winking at me, or so the mind is wired to think.

I went on to tell him that I had begun to learn that home is not so much a particular place as it is something we can take with us through our human relationships and our connection to God. And then Mead told me the perfect story. A fourth-century Greek Orthodox bishop named St. Basil of Caesarea had been threatened with exile by a tyrant. St. Basil responded to the threats as follows: "Exile will be impossible, since everywhere on God's earth I am at home." The tyrant was so impressed that he did not exile St. Basil after all. As I left, Mead said, "I bet ten years from now, if you ever end up back in Cleveland, it will feel a little strange to you." He was probably right. That was a terrifically astute pastoral comment to leave me with.

I had wandered into this church and just felt the urge to talk to this stranger about all that was on my mind. And it so happened that he empathized deeply, because he had moved at about the same age as my son and shared the name Andrew. I took this as God's gift, as an experience of God's love through another person. Our national survey indicates that most Americans do have this sense that God's love inspires other people to connect with us at times. The encounter with Rev. Andrew Mead was somewhat confirming of this move. People are wired to want that confirmation. People look for God-winks, little signs that God is with them behind the scenes. I wanted to close the gap of dissonance between where

I had been and where I was and where I was headed. I was looking for spiritual glue between past, present, and future. I wanted some shooting star in the night sky with my name on it intended to convey a message from above that all is well. This is not crazy; this is human. We are all meaning-making creatures, inclined to find purpose and intention behind things.

Let me offer another God-wink—one that tells me that even two years after our move, knowing that Andrew was doing just fine, God knew I needed a little reassurance. In May 2010, I was visiting the Fetzer Institute in Kalamazoo, Michigan, to speak with the leaders of the institute's National Love and Forgiveness Campaign. There were about thirty people there from each region of the country, all of them leaders in encouraging love, compassion, and forgiveness in their cities and towns. I sat down for lunch with Shirley Showalter, then Fetzer vice president for programs. She asked me how Stony Brook was going, and we agreed that it was a good thing for me to have taken on a leadership role there in the field of compassionate care. She asked how the family was doing, and I mentioned that we were all fine now, but that it took Mom and Dad longer to adjust than young Andrew. She smiled as if she knew something.

Shirley told me that when she was thirteen, her family moved from one town to another, and she had to change schools. She had just been drifting along in life, without much identity, and she hadn't been an especially good student. But her first assignment happened to be a text she had already read and studied the month before, in her old school. She did so well that her teacher called her "a brain." As it happened, it was "cooler" to be smart in her new school than it was in her previous school. As a cool kid, she cultivated a new self-image that shaped her life as she eventually became a college president at a distinguished Mennonite school in northern Indiana. So moving was for her a positive, life-changing experience.

The Fetzer Institute is an amazingly spiritual place, and I was not surprised to feel that somehow the universe had set up this little lunch conversation, although I understood that my brain was an active partner in my perceptions. What I call God-winks and grace notes, psychologists term "confirmation bias." Cognitive scientists tell us that this bias is ineradicably engrained in our nature. Those who study the evolution of the mind tell us that religion itself is partly the result of our being neurologically wired to see the world as teleological—as purposeful—because this is a confirmation of our being. I believe that the greatest human need is the need for significance. We human beings need this safety, and that is why we have always tended to attribute divine significance to commonplace events, reconstructed as uncommon. Some scientists say that prayer evolved as a way in which we internally prime ourselves for a sign. We begin to have a heightened sensitivity for deeper meaning and awareness, and for that I am grateful.

I can recall being on an Amtrak train headed north from Washington a few years back. I had been thinking and praying about finding a new book agent. I opened my eyes, and there across the aisle was a woman reading a big, thick manuscript with a pen in her hand, marking it up here and there. She looked like a real professional. I politely asked her what she was up to. It turned out that she was a book agent, the kind who really cares about the writing careers of the people she takes on. We exchanged cards. That was Loretta Barrett of Loretta Barrett Books, who became my agent. She is thoughtful and enjoyable and concerned and honest, and gets the spiritual side of life.

Just one more wink. In 1985, we were moving from Ann Arbor to Tarrytown for a new teaching job. Wow! That move was a bit of a hard time, too. I had to spend nearly every penny of my first paycheck just to get into an apartment in Tarrytown—and then there was nothing to do but wait for the next paycheck. Meanwhile, we were running low on food for us and our then two-year-old daughter. Mitsuko and I found ourselves sitting in our car in the parking lot of a Howard Johnson's just near the east entrance to the Tappan Zee Bridge, counting our pennies to see what kind of lunch we could scrape up for all of us. We were feeling pretty desperate. At that point, we closed our eyes and prayed for someone to just flat out give us $100 to hold us over until the check arrived. *Bump!* The car shook a tiny bit. We opened our eyes, and I got out to see what was going on. This huge guy came running up to me, smiling apologetically. "Sorry," he said, pointing to his Cadillac. "I think I may have tapped the corner of your car. But no damage, right? Why don't you just take this?" And with that, he handed me a $100 bill. I told the man that he was literally the answer to a prayer, that our car was pretty beat up anyway, and that we were going to take our daughter into HoJo's and have a great lunch. He laughed and said, "Great!" Mitsuko and I breathed an enormous, collective sigh of relief and felt our stress melt away. A few days later, my paycheck arrived in the mail.

COMPASSION AND FORGIVENESS

Suffering is inevitable in life. We never need to look for it because it is looking for us, and at some point it finds us. How do we deal with it? I believe that God really does use suffering to break us down without ever truly breaking us fully, in order to encourage humility and growth. We are like seeds planted in the soil, unable to grow until the outer shell is broken by a loving power that wants us to become better.

At Christmas in 2009, I received two special cards. One was from my high school theology teacher, Rev. Rod Welles, who wrote that although he had spent much of his life elsewhere, he had returned to his native Wilmington, and that it had worked out rather well. Another, from the artist Cathie Beck of Cleveland Heights, read, "I have found on my moves prior to Cleveland that it takes at least two years before I feel comfortable in the new city."

The compassion of both my old friends came shining through, and made me more accepting of the naturalness of some of my feelings. Whatever peaks and valleys this move created for us, these just came with territory, and no one could be blamed, really.

But I did need to do a little forgiving, and sometimes only time really heals. Thank heavens for forgetfulness! But if a friend like Jim LaRue can forgive the man who tortured, raped, and murdered his daughter Molly—despite the fact that he says "the hole in my heart from her loss remains"—so are we all capable of forgiveness. He read his letter of forgiveness to me in the Cedar-Fairmont Starbucks in Cleveland Heights a few days before he headed off in his old car for the drive to New Bloomfield, Pennsylvania, where he would read it in court the following afternoon in the presence of the man who killed Molly and her fiancé. It is one of the most powerful statements of compassion, forgiveness, and unlimited love that I have ever heard:

> I am very pleased that your death sentences have been replaced with life imprisonment without chance of parole. However horrible your actions, I do not believe in the death penalty which is an act of vengeance, even if it is state authorized. Vengeance is never an answer to anything. It only breeds more violence and more retribution.
>
> And so, Paul, I am here today to offer you forgiveness for what you have done.
>
> I wish that you and I can now find peace.
>
> What do I ask of you for this offering of forgiveness. Nothing! It is freely given.
>
> But I do offer you a suggestion. With the death penalty no longer hanging over you, I hope that you will be able to find

significant meaning in your life. Your mind and spirit can never be imprisoned. There are a growing number of serial killers in the country. My family has always believed that discovering the pain and fear that caused the violence could foster understanding and make us all more genuinely human. I hope you will consider accepting counsel from those who can help you understand what caused you to commit acts of violence and how you might help other troubled people.

Molly had decided to devote her life to working with troubled children, like you certainly were. She was determined to find out why these kids acted out in terribly violent ways. She was convinced that if you could reach them at an early enough stage of their development, they could find their way through the circumstances that seemed to be driving them to violent ends. She would have wanted that for you.

Paul, I think it would be great if you could pick up where Molly left off, starting with yourself. Help the Molly's of this world learn who you are and try to enlist the help of other inmates to help in this effort. You are a gold mine of critical information that needs to be unearthed.

I can assure you Paul, that Molly will be with you every step of the way. Because that is how much she cares!!

Peace be with you. Peace be with you.

When Jim read this, Paul looked up when the word "forgiveness" was uttered, and he continued to make eye contact.

I also think of Pastor Otis Moss when it comes to forgiveness. In the 1990s, I reconnected with the African American tradition of *agape* love as a holy emotion through the remarkable Moss, a spiritual mentor for so many people, including Oprah Winfrey. Just being around Moss, one senses his quiet emotional depth of heart. Rev. Gary Davis, Rev. John T. Walker, and Rev. Otis Moss were three wonderful teachers, and I am privileged to still enjoy an abiding friendship with Moss, for the other two men are long since deceased. These great men used the language of *agape* love boldly. They understood that Unlimited Love is the basis of everything, from the glue that holds the universe together to the practice of nonviolent resistance as a moral and spiritual political practice. Such African American pastors and thinkers were part of the most surprising force in social change in the past century of America.

During his early days as a minister, Moss was blessed to sit within the inner circle of many phenomenal persons, such as Benjamin E. Mays and Martin Luther King Jr. Both of these men provided friendship, leadership, and spiritual guidance and helped shape the thinking and model of leadership that Moss represents today. He served as copastor with Martin Luther King Sr. at Ebenezer Baptist Church in Atlanta. He is recognized across the nation and globe as a charismatic and spiritual man of God, carrying the banner of justice and equality in civil rights for all.

In 2005, I asked Moss what message he had for today's troubled youth. I think his answer is really a message for all of us: "There is no substitute for excellence, and there is absolutely no substitute for unconditional love, transforming love, *agape* love, unlimited love, and that it is the most radical, the most transforming force in the universe. And it is the most empowering reality in the universe. If you want to be powerful, you've got to learn how to love. And if you want to be courageous, you've got to learn how to forgive. And if you want to be *completely* human, you've got to learn the values and the moral demands of reconciliation. And it is possible."

To which I say, amen.

In the end, I am like most people in relying on spirituality in hard times. How does one maintain a quiet mind, clear and calm, from which positive thoughts and actions can proceed? The stresses of our move were disturbing for us at the heart level, with the circuits of mental worry giving rise to tiredness and stress. We had to call on the deepest and most positive qualities within ourselves. These qualities—benevolent love, beauty, truth, gratitude, hope, joy, noble purpose, awe, creativity—are natural to all of us and lie at the core of our being. But to find them, we had to control the negative qualities that had been dug up along with our roots, and which sometimes obscured what we knew to be true. We were going through the eye of the needle.

In easy times, we can be optimistic and happy and can move ahead in our routines, without feeling the need to call on God's love to help us. But in hard times, when we are dealing with lots of emotional, relational, and environmental stressors, many people really do need spirituality. They always have and they always will, whatever the latest atheistic best seller. We need some sense that at the center of our own being is a point of contact with a Higher Power that has things in control when we don't and who sees the light at the end of the tunnel when we can't quite make it out. Without spirituality, we all too easily forget who we are. In this life, when we become disoriented and are perhaps on the brink of despair, we can find a hidden door that opens on a path of ascent that we never imagined before. We can find the link between a temporal and material world and the world of spiritual emotions and eternity. In this is a peace that passes all understanding. We can then stand in courage as points of light, and bring healing to ourselves, our families, and the world.

By the way, for those who do not believe in God, it is still possible to affirm that if there were a deity worthy of worship, it would be essentially a manifestation in the highest form of all the unselfish loves that we express in our lives and know to be the very essence of human thriving.

 FINDING YOUR OWN HIDDEN GIFTS
Compassion and Unlimited Love

Love is not just a feeling to be hidden away in the heart and enjoyed privately. Love is something we show in everything we say and do, a witness to our families, our friends, and the world.

- **Look for God-winks and grace notes.** The world is a very different place depending on how you look at it. Instead of seeing events in your life as random and unconnected, actively look for the meaningful coincidences and lessons life brings you. I assure you, the pattern will emerge sooner or later!

- **Be open to surprises.** Life inevitably happens to us, despite our excellent plans, our noble purpose, and our clear vision of the future. But most of our success comes from responding to unexpected people, events, and opportunities. Respond creatively to all the things that just find you in life—meeting someone who shares your dreams, accepting the offer of a free music lesson, taking a new job on a hunch. Listen to the world around you, and have a sense that beneath the surface of so many surprising encounters there is a God of love. Surprises are where the good things happen.

- **Answer the big four items of the divine love scale.** Take a moment to answer these questions about your relationship to God's love. How you score is not a judgment but a reflection of your relationship today. If your scores are mostly d's, e's, and f's, consider it a blessing. If not, stay open to God-winks, grace notes, and surprises!

1. I feel God's love as the greatest power in the universe.
   a. Never (or I don't believe in God)
   b. Once in a while
   c. Some days
   d. Most days
   e. Every day
   f. More than once a day

2. I feel God's love directly.
   a. Never (or I don't believe in God)
   b. Once in a while
   c. Some days
   d. Most days
   e. Every day
   f. More than once a day

3. I feel God's love through others.
   a. Never (or I don't believe in God)
   b. Once in a while
   c. Some days
   d. Most days
   e. Every day
   f. More than once a day

4. I feel God's love increasing my compassion for others.
   a. Never (or I don't believe in God)
   b. Once in a while
   c. Some days
   d. Most days
   e. Every day
   f. More than once a day

6

The Gift of Hope

Hope completes the circle: every act of self-giving, love, and compassion gives birth to hope. Hope is love's greatest gift. My wife, Mitsuko, always finds hope in her garden.

Love of the earth runs in Mitsuko's blood. She was born on a rice farm in a small village in remote northern Japan. She later went to classical Japanese dancing school, and eventually traveled to New York to perform. We met after one of those performances many years ago, and were married in Hyde Park, Chicago, in 1982. So for Mitsuko, our move was a continuation of the complex emotional journey across worlds she had begun years ago. In the process, she has learned to take her sense of home with her, wherever she goes. And the best expression of home for her is her garden. Like her mother before her, Mitsuko is of the earth, full of wonder at the things she grows. In Japan, people see the earth and its fruits in mystical terms, and it is clear that underneath all this earth and planting, she sees a hint of the divine at work.

Every seed is a symbol of rebirth. And that was just what we needed.

For many years Mitsuko had a big garden in Shaker Heights where she grew enough vegetables to feed our family and some of the neighbors through the summer months. When we bought the new house in Setauket, she dug a big new garden right away—about twenty feet by twenty-five feet. As the losses of the move washed over her, she engaged more and more deeply in her gardening. Sometimes she would spend half the day out there, working in the soil. She was celebrating nature, creative growth, and hope in this immense love of the earth and its fruits. Creative growth is always a symbol of hope, and the hopeful symbol of a garden remains the same whether in Ohio or out on Long Island. The earth and its fruits are the same wherever you are. Mitsuko was so busy growing things and giving vegetables to neighbors that she had no time to get caught up in self-doubt. Her gardening was an act of love, hope, and resilience all in one. She was growing roots when we were feeling uprooted.

The relationship between gardens and hope is an old theme, going right back to Eden. Like Sam in *The Lord of the Rings*, gardeners seem to find it easier to get back in touch with the ground of their being after a long voyage. In growing a garden, Mitsuko found a way to control her circumstances and assert her abilities to create something beautiful. She loves those green peppers and tomatoes, and is thrilled when the first ones are on the table. And so are we.

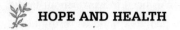

HOPE AND HEALTH

I am not a gardener, but I am glad that Mitsuko is. And it isn't just for the good food. Hope makes a difference in a woman's health over the long run. Dr. Hilary Tindle and other Women's Health Initiative investigators found that optimistic and pessimistic attitudes affect coronary heart disease and mortality in postmenopausal women.[1] Women with positive future expectations had lower rates of heart disease and total mortality than those who were despairing.

Getting to hope is physiologically important, and it may be that the benefits of the helper therapy principle are mediated in part by the elevation of hope that the principle allows. Consider that placebos are oftentimes almost as effective as real medications, and that a good portion of the impact of many medicines—about 30 to 40 percent on average—is attributable to our hope in them. A 2002 review of current literature on hope and its effects lists a wide variety of scientific publications linking hope with coping with arthritis, recovering from major burns, reducing pain from spinal cord injuries, and so forth.[2] Hope creates a series of physiological interactions that we are only beginning to appreciate.[3]

Of course, all of this benefit exists only within limits, and we should never think that health so rests on the cultivation of hope that being diagnosed with a serious disease or not recovering from it is somehow the result of our failure to hope enough. In fact, we are all frail and mortal creatures. Still, despair is not a healthy thing. We need to worry about losing hope ourselves, and about the people around us losing hope. So much of leadership in a family or on the job is about modeling hope.

🌿 HANGING ON TO HOPE

We all need a garden of hope in life's challenging periods— real hope, the kind that grows deep roots.

This hope is different from mere optimism. Optimism is easy and smiley-faced (though there is nothing wrong with staying on the sunny side). And it is also different from mere expectation—the point of expecting anything is that it is more or less already on the way, and can be anticipated. But deep hope—the conviction that despite everything, things will somehow work out—is a much more intentional thing that takes more work. It is a leaning into the future with a trust that something good will eventually come. When things are going well, optimism is good enough. But in hard times, we need hope. Think about it: we can pray for the strength to hope, but no one prays for mere optimism!

By its nature, hope is more irrational than rational, and it has to be stubborn enough to redefine reality. In a life where every hope is crushed again and again, hope can be defeated for a while, and maybe even forever, though I don't believe it. A few years ago I received a heartbreaking letter from a woman named Ambrosia, a prisoner in Texas who had clearly given up hope. She wrote, "I sit here in prison sick from various illnesses and unable to receive proper medical care because I'm a no good scum of the earth criminal in the eyes of certain people. . . . I loved my prostitute mother even though she didn't love me. I loved my junkie father, even though he never loved me. I loved my abusive grandfather even after he beat me, told me I was no good, abused my young body, my young mind. I loved them all unconditionally, unselfish, wanting nothing in return. Now 41 years later who will love this broken spirit, broken woman dying in prison because of people who continue to abuse me? I don't believe there is such a thing as 'Altruistic Love.'"

I responded to Ambrosia that despite all, she can still find love and hope when the time is right. I mentioned Louisiana's Angola Prison, a maximum-security prison with a population of lifers, almost all of whom have committed murder. Now there is a hospice in the prison for these inmates as they grow old and face death. The prisoners volunteer to be compassionate caregivers of individuals in the hospice. With this new role, these prisoners seem to light up with hope and with meaning. Many say that while they were growing up they experienced things that were as harsh as what Ambrosia went through. But somehow, as the years passed by and they mellowed with age, they found as much of a connection between hope and the care of others as anyone else in life. We always have hope so long as we have the capacity to give, but we do start out at different points on the curve depending on the circumstances we have to confront as children, when we are most easily injured.

I also mentioned to Ambrosia some prisoners I had known at the Grafton Correctional Institute not far from Oberlin, Ohio; people who in the heat of passion, in the lust for revenge, or in the daze of drunkenness killed another human being. A lot of these men also came from very difficult backgrounds. The ones who seemed to have overcome their difficulties and who had the most cheer and hope in life were the ones who volunteered with the prison farm. They grew crops and raised a small herd of cattle that were used to provide food not just for other prisoners but for the neediest. These men, sometimes as many as forty gathered together for an evening meeting, would give remarkable testimony about how this small activity of helping others liberated them into a whole new level of purpose and hope. They were not hoping for parole, because the nature of their crimes was so serious. But they found hope in the opportunity to give back to society and to assume a positive role. So I have seen compassion come alive in prison, and I know that it can be nurtured. I suggested that no matter what she had been through, no matter how hard her experiences had been, she still could benefit from getting involved in some organized volunteering around the prison; and that even if she did this grudgingly at first, there was a good chance that she would eventually find it very gratifying.

I never heard from Ambrosia again, but I hold hope for her. Maybe I have read too much Dostoyevsky. The Russian writer is popular among theologians because he thought that no matter how shadowy and harsh life might become, and no matter how despicable our own actions might be, there is always this hope for a spiritual transformation. He did not diminish the reality of the shadows, or think that the grief and losses in life and opportunity were not deep and devastating. He certainly understood the way the human mind gets caught up in horrid emotions and darkness. But he felt that in any of us, change is possible. I hope Ambrosia experiences this.

In July 2010, I noted an e-mail that came my way from one Allison Granger-Brown of Vancouver, Canada. She wrote, "I help create opportunities for women in prison to help others and know that it is the earliest indicator of their commitment to their own healing. Amongst other programs, we are currently collating beads and making cards to send to women in prison in Nairobi. These opportunities are always freely chosen and so only the women who are moved to help become engaged. I hope you come to visit our city again and share with us your recent research and learning journey. If you ever consider a prison talk we would be honoured to host you." I took this e-mail as hopeful, and I keep my fingers crossed for Ambrosia.

In my town of Setauket, in my former home city of Cleveland, and all over the United States, a lot of people are in a prison of sorts. Our nation is not doing well on the international happiness rankings. The problem is one of diminished community and spiritual emptiness. We try to fill in this emptiness with extra trips to the mall, the cathedrals of the modern world where we see people and feel a part of the action but know no one. We place our emphasis on things rather than on the great spiritual emotions of awe, wonder, noble purpose, meaning, faith, self-control, wisdom, selfless love, forgiveness, service, simple kindness, and the like. And we struggle to find the right communities, schools, houses of worship, workplaces, and environments to foster these great perennial spiritual values.

Many Americans these days are learning hard lessons. A lot of folks are unemployed, and many of those jobs are not going to return for a long time, if ever. Pension funds are breaking down. People my age who have been financially comfortable for years suddenly face a more complex future. For the first time in American history, it seems likely that children will not be better off financially than their parents, and many may be worse off with levels of taxation that sap the will to succeed. We are a country in significant degree owned by China, the national deficit is out of control, and politicians are ineffective. It is pretty terrifying to buy a house for a lot of money and then see its value decline radically to the point of being "underwater." Wars, clashes of cultures, hate-mongers, mad bombers. Earthquakes devastate places like Haiti and Chile, tsunamis swamp Thailand, storms destroy Samoa, hurricanes flood New Orleans. The ground beneath our feet feels shaky. The answers can no longer come from politics, but from within each individual. What lies ahead of us can only be managed by drawing out the compassion that lies within us.

So where is hope? Around the edges of these bad things there have to be opportunities for growth, *and there always are*, categorically and without exception. Life is hard and very hard. There are things we rightly fear in every stage of life.

I do not want to suggest for a moment that bad and hard things are not *really* bad and hard. All I am saying is that around these edges is opportunity for growth and hope through giving. No matter how hard the times, there is always something or someone to be thankful for, including the one person who seems to understand what we are experiencing and can offer a listening presence by just being there with us a bit. There is always reason to hope, and there is always a way back to hope in the darkest times.

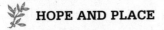 ## HOPE AND PLACE

How we interact with a new environment and with the people in that environment will influence our state of hope. We silly philosophers think of our minds as unaffected by place, when in fact even creativity itself, as researcher Esther Sternberg has demonstrated, is significantly enhanced by inspiring environments and proximity to natural vistas.[4] The Enlightenment idea that our minds and creativity are separate from place and people constitutes the false myth of the solitary one for whom the external world is irrelevant.

Here along the North Shore of Long Island, I have some favorite views from the hills looking over the Long Island Sound, and I do grab that ferry from Port Jefferson to Bridgeport rather than confront the traffic on the Long Island Expressway, even though it's cheaper to drive over the bridge to get to Connecticut. A while ago, when returning from Providence, Rhode Island, I took the ferry from New London to Orient Point on the very end of Long Island, and that was even more inspiring. I know it feels good to be on the water, sipping tea and watching the waves. The ride gets me away from the background noise of phones and separates me from endless e-mail. Mostly, the beauty helps me write, and I always have my laptop open. In fact, studies show that a beautiful place and the related serenity increase our creativity when it comes to questions that require the integrative bringing together of ideas from different domains of the mind.[5] So I find hope looking out over those waves.

It strikes me that if a human being were truly without hope, he or she would no longer be able to live. Objectively, life does not always lend itself to hope. We are born without our consent and spend a lot of time figuring out how to make ends meet. We don't have much control over most things. Perhaps that's why our minds are hardwired to tune out most of life's uncertainties. Otherwise we would be anxious around the clock and never sleep. That person driving in front of us could be drunk or have a heart attack and veer over into our lane. Our own heart can stop beating any second. When young we fear the absence of parents or the inevitable screaming arguments between Mom and Dad, as adolescents we fear rejection by our peers, as young adults we fear not getting a good job to start off in life or not finding a spouse, as middle-aged adults we are anxious about our teenage kids trying to grow up in modern American culture, and as we grow older we fear the inevitable diagnosis of severe and eventually life-threatening illness or the loss of a pension plan.

Nature's beauty can be a window into hope, as can a beautiful work of art or music. But for me, the ultimate place of beauty is the human heart, visible in small actions of helping others. Beauty is in our human nature if we allow it to breathe, and it can withstand all those mishaps of life that leave us honestly asking if hope is just too irrational, given the evidence. Hope rests in the beauty of lives lived in harmony with others as well as with the natural environment. When I am around someone whose heart is really radiant and energetic and peaceful, as seen in an abidingly joyful facial expression that is not changed by circumstances and seems to be grounded in something eternal, I am without exception around someone who has discovered the giver's glow. Such individuals have, despite all the miserable scenes of hatred and indifference in the drama of life, found a way to be beautifully defiant in a hope that is inextricably bound up with self-giving. Their hope is not so much about the "doing" of things, in having certain goals and pursuing them across chronological time from present to future. Their hope is in their very "being," it is in eternal time, it is between them and their God, and it is in the very activity of self-giving love in the pure present.

So the heart, and not our location on the face of the earth, is ultimately *the* place where we dwell. The key to hope is focusing our minds and hearts inwardly on the ways and power of love so as to reflect this focus in our relationships with others. It does not take too much time to hear the call of our hearts, and it is the only call that makes our species worth struggling for. It does take a spiritual exercise of some type, whether prayer, meditation, or visualization—and all three can go together—to establish this focus; and during the course of our busy day it is imperative to pause, breathe deep, and affirm this focus. Such practices can bring hope and positivity into our lives anywhere. For Victor Frankl, small acts of self-giving love were the source of a hope that enabled him to endure a concentration camp; for Abraham Lincoln, it was sustained self-giving love that brought him some relief from the chronic melancholy that plagued him over the years. There is a special beauty in such hope.

I worry about hope when we are constantly caught up in the sensate images we see on our televisions, on our computer screens, in the letters of text messages, in the interconnected worlds of social media. And yet this meta-world of the Internet is a place as well, and we have access to it wherever we are. In so many ways, this world constitutes our place and location and we have it wherever we move to. And that can be a life-saver. But these virtual connections do not sustain themselves in the absence of real interactions. And I wonder if all this attention to a network of electronic images, which is some-times so captivating that we can so easily ignore the real world of social relations around us, is diverting us from the beauty and hope that reside inwardly in our hearts. The jury is still out on this one, and there are pessimists and optimists. How, when we live such distracting lives, do we close the motorways of our senses to focus within? Is there time left to take a few moments to breathe in and cultivate calmness and tranquility from within?

So, hope and place. We live in this place, with these familiar sites and visions, and with this history of social connectivity and relational capital. We find hope in the wonders of the natural world and in the awesome beauty of the human heart at its joyous best. But staying in touch with that joyous best—that is the most important goal of life for anyone and for everyone. This is where true beauty resides, and it is a beauty as astounding as any we find in music or in art. It is worth taking the time to relax and get free of tense and anxious thoughts and tap into the pure energies of the heart.

HOPE AT BROOKE'S PLACE

When I arrived in Stony Brook, one of my old friends mentioned that I should get to know a local woman, Brooke M. Ellison, the subject of the astonishing movie *The Brooke Ellison Story*, produced by the late Christopher Reeve.[6] Brooke became quadriplegic in a traffic accident that occurred just a mile down the road from my office. This remarkable young woman went on to graduate from Harvard, where she gave the student commencement speech for which she was featured on the front page of the *New York Times*.

When I first called Brooke and mentioned a mutual friend's suggestion that we get together, she generously invited me over to her home, where I met her amazing parents, Jean and Ed, at the door. I think that Brooke and her family are a living tribute to the connection between love and hope. Brooke was completely impossible to feel sorry for as she called over from her wheelchair, with an amazing array of technology surrounding her body. In that wheelchair I saw the power of love and hope at work in a young woman who had clearly dug down into the deep spiritual wells of the heart in a way that few others are challenged to do. All around were photographs of her friends—Brooke with Christopher Reeve, with Bill Clinton, with her Harvard classmates, with so many people who found hope in her life. Her home was itself a testimony to a father's love, as the backyard was one big wooden porch allowing perfect access for Brooke to connect with the nature around her.

I began to visit with Brooke about once a week or so, usually in the evenings for an hour or two, and we now teach a course for the medical students about how to encourage hope in the lives of patients. I first thought of visiting Brooke as an act of kindness, but I quickly discovered that it was the beginning of one of my most prized friendships here. Brooke has an appointment in our Center now, helping medical students think about how to relate to patients and families with hope and compassion, and doing hope research with me.

Here are Brooke's own words, written with the aid of an intricate computer system that she controls with a small electronic device under her tongue:

In September of 1990, when I was eleven years old, I was hit by a car while walking home from my first day of seventh-grade. That accident altered my life immeasurably, both physically and emotionally, as it left me paralyzed from my neck down and dependent on a ventilator to breathe. There are no lessons to be learned that can adequately prepare someone for an event like this, and it is a set of circumstances that only begins to become normal over time. However, there might not be any more significant or personally satisfying means to make this transition from utter abnormality to normality than through using the events in our lives to make the adjustment more bearable in someone else's. It is through the giving of hope to someone else that we, in turn, receive it, ourselves. It is with this in mind that I share the story of my relationship with Amanda.

After having lived for over fifteen years with quadriplegia, I was told of a young girl, Amanda, who was injured in an automobile accident, leaving her similarly paralyzed and dependent on a ventilator. At the age of eight, Amanda not only suffered physically but also suffered emotionally, with feelings of anger, depression, and frustration, so much so that she did not want to interact with the world or even be a part of it. I was approached in the hopes that my life as I had lived it could prove helpful to Amanda as she adjusted to her new life.

In the years since I have known her, I have seen Amanda evolve from a position of near despair to one of contentment and hope. I couldn't possibly claim sole credit for this evolution, but what I can claim is a greater sense of hope in my own life as a result of my relationship with her. However much I have given to Amanda through my own understandings about life and challenge, I know without equivocation that I have received just as much.

Through my relationship with Amanda, and with so many others who have touched my life over the years, I have come to realize that it isn't the nature of the challenges we face that make us who we are but, instead, what we learn to do with these challenges and how we make them meaningful both in our own lives and in others. I also have come to understand that giving and receiving hope are only separated by semantics, and that they are nearly mirror images. When we instill hope in those who need it, we find it for ourselves just the same, and there is no greater gift than that.

Brooke herself is a place of hope and self-giving. Perhaps one of the most important gifts she gives is her being a role model for all of us to transcend our circumstances and hardships in a powerful way, blowing right through them to get in touch with that which alone makes human lives noble and dignified. Hardships do not have to mean the end of hope, but rather can mean the beginning, especially if we can discover the power of self-giving as a way of defying despair. Be part of some cause larger than self, with which you feel a special affinity, and focus your service there with special depth and commitment. Self alone is a pretty meager proposition.

✿ A GOOD AND HOPEFUL VISION

When we think we have lost everything, how is it possible to still have hope? Just as we have a first aid kit in the house in case of emergency, having a basic set of spiritual values—compassionate love, the habit of giving to others, a higher purpose that guides us, and plain and simple gratitude—will always help us flourish. Applying these remedies to the things that have hurt our souls will give us the most important gift of all: a good and hopeful vision of what can be. It is this hope that keeps us alive and keeps us walking on our journeys, no matter how difficult they are. Do you have a vision for your life? You cannot live well without one. Proverbs 29:18 reads, "Where there is no vision the people perish."

Hope is perhaps as simple as deciding to be open to surprises in life, things around the corner that we cannot predict and that come into our lives unexpectedly. I like to recall the day in June 2001, when I was sitting in my office at Case Western and received a fax from Sir John Templeton. He said he wanted to found a research institute focused not on human deficits and disease but on human strengths and assets, and especially on the practice of self-giving love, people's sense that love underlies the universe, and love's relation to faith and hope. I faxed back asking him what we might call such an institute. His response was immediate: we should call it the Institute for Research on Unlimited Love. He believed in the idea of *agape* love, the Greek word for a love that is unconditional and inspired from above. But in a world where not too many people speak Greek, he thought "unlimited" would do the job.

I experienced a moment of trepidation. I faxed back, "Sir John, how about an Institute for Creative Altruism?" I thought perhaps "altruism" would sound more scientific. But Sir John would not be deterred from his vision. "I think Unlimited Love," he responded, and indicated he was ready to commit several million dollars to an institute of that name. I faxed back, "Sir John, that is my kind of language. It jumps right off the page."

He was right, of course, because love really is the whole basis of a good vision. It is the crowning glory of every life, the ultimate source of the meaning, dignity, hope, and deep happiness that we mortal and frail creatures seek. Botox, anabolic steroids, human growth hormone, all the dubious promises of a fountain of youth—all are for sale, but none add to our dignity or happiness. The capacity for a generous love already lies within us waiting only to be more fully unveiled and actively engaged.

Hope is not simply the capacity to be optimistic; it is so much bigger than that. Hope leads us into the future with a deep trust that something good will come. It helps us keep going when we stumble, and gives us a vision to guide us in the face of adversity.

KEEPING THE VISION

Life really can become what we envision, although sometimes it takes others to point that out to us. A highly regarded leader of pastoral care at the Stony Brook Hospital, Rev. Steve Unger, sat down with me the day before Thanksgiving of 2009, and said that the program we were building really seemed to be making a difference in people's attitudes and lives. The chair of family medicine, Jeff Trilling, stopped me in the hall and said that same thing. They said that our positivity had really lifted up a lot of people. So maybe this is a big silver lining—I was here, after all, to make a difference in this place, in this time, albeit for reasons that remained a little unclear.

Everything that comes into being started as a thought, and everything great and innovative started with a vision. With the right vision, diligent dedication, and perseverance, we can succeed one small step at a time, bit by bit, with a goal in mind. If we don't know what we want to achieve, we probably won't achieve it. We had a vision for a new center in a major university and medical school, one focused on education and research in compassionate and humanistic care. Vision is a big piece of spiritual capital, and it sure gave us the sense of purpose to do well.

As I began to feel that I really was working toward this vision, I shifted in the direction of gratitude. Though uprooted, I was becoming a better leader and a more compassionate person, more sensitive to the quiet desperation felt by others, especially when they were adjusting to a big move. I was grateful for Elisa Nelson, my administrative partner, because so much of the good that came of this move came because of her loyalty, good judgment, and hospitality. There is a reason why hospitality to the stranger is so central to the moral precepts of the Hebrew Bible. And I was grateful to Dean Richard N. Fine for sticking with the plan in times of economic woe, and for then president Shirley Strum Kenny. Recruiting excellent faculty made me grateful to them. I was especially tuned into their transition issues, and that really yanked me beyond my own self and anxieties. They were going through some of the things that I had experienced. These were folks I would pray for and be supportive of, and about whom I cared greatly. So my own transition issues receded into the background. This was, again, the helper therapy principle in action.

Every act of giving is an act of hope. Focus on giving behavior that draws on your talents and strengths, and strive to do it more often. The great African American theologian Howard Thurman wrote, "Don't ask yourself what the world needs. Ask yourself what makes you come alive and then go do that. Because what the world needs is people who have come alive."[7] Do "unto others" with your most wonderful gifts, using the talents that bring out the best in you. You need not try to be what you are not. There are others who have the gifts that you do not.

You can become hopeful by being a giver right where you are, at any time. You don't have to be a Mother Teresa to be a giving person. Even she said, "We can do no great things; only small things with great love." Helen Keller and numerous others have made the same point. St. Paul had it right: "We are God's workmanship, created in Christ Jesus to do good works, which God prepared in advance for us to do" (Ephesians 2:10). It is in this "workmanship" that we are made to do good and from which the giver's glow arises, and it is in this that we see in the human substrate a hint of the hopes of God.

St. Paul wrote, "God loves a cheerful giver" (2 Corinthians 9:7). He wrote also that the compassionate have the gift of "cheerfulness" (Romans 12:8). Human nature has a substrate of goodness and love of others that is to be celebrated, that helps us get through hard times, and that makes life worth living.

Despite our differences, we can work together to transform our lives from self-centeredness to a spirituality and practice of helping others, of compassionate love, of kindness. For me, a sense that we have a divine partner luring us in this direction despite our hesitancy is important when the shadows of human nature block out the light, but always only for the nonce.

"Love never fails" (1 Corinthians, 13:8), and we can never let it fail.

🌿 FINDING YOUR OWN HIDDEN GIFTS
Hope

For me, hope is intertwined with my belief in a loving God who has purposes for our lives. To give up on hope would be to give up on God. In hard times, we learn that faith, hope, and love are woven together into the fabric of endurance. Love makes hope possible; hope makes love possible. Both are acts of defiance against tough times. They are both about active agency, choice, self-control. There is a lot of suffering in life, and how we will respond to it is our choice. Hard times either make us or break us, and that's up to us and no one else. We can choose to be consumed by sorrows and regrets, or we can practice the healing vision of hope.

- **Celebrate what you have already achieved.** So often, when we feel that we are losing ground or drifting away from the life we thought we wanted, we forget the good things we have done in life. If we're lucky, someone points out to us how well we've done in the past, and encourages us to keep plugging. Ask your friends and family to help you remember all that you've already achieved. If there's no one around to ask, free your mind of negative thoughts long enough to let your higher self speak the truth to you.
- **Find your vision.** The American mystic Charles Fillmore, founder of the Unity Church, wrote, "Thoughts are things." Your life really does become what you envision. In hard times, when life feels out of control, the right affirmations spoken aloud or inwardly contemplated can be a way to retain mastery over your inner self. Put aside your negative thoughts and fears, and look into the crystal ball of your perfect world: What is your best vision for your future? Where do you really want to be? What do you really want to be doing? You are what you think.
- **Practice spirituality.** Material things do matter, of course, but they rest on a deep and firm foundation of spirituality. Place your hope not so much in getting a better house or winning the lottery but in positive spiritual emotions that have healing power for others and for yourself. Cultivate a spirituality of hope, gratitude, compassion, creativity, mirth, joy, inner freedom, and inner peace.

Always Coming Home

Twenty-one months after we moved from Cleveland to Setauket, I asked my son, Drew—no longer Andrew, and suddenly six feet tall—if there was one quotation from him that he would like to see in this book. He responded instantly in his now deep voice, and with conviction, "Yeah—this move was the best decision of my life."

"Anything else?" I asked, and waited.

"Yeah," he said. "When you get a chance to move in life, it can be a great thing."

When we first arrived on these shores in the middle of a driving storm, my young son was fuming with anger, and rightly so. Frankly, I had no idea how all this would impact him or any of us. Maybe it would bring out the very best in my son, or maybe it would be a lot more harmful than we ever imagined. This was a big sacrifice for him, and there wasn't any choice involved. In those early months, as we made the trek back to Cleveland for long weekends once a month, he was becoming a New Yorker.

Drew recreated himself here in Setauket, and he has grown in a lot of ways, all of them good. The first month here I would take Drew over to the Mount Sinai skateboarding park, and that helped out. But once he began school, he dropped that part of himself cold. It was just not in keeping with his self-image anymore. First of all, Andrew became Drew. He allowed the much-discussed earring hole in his left ear to close, and transformed step by step over the months into a great student, a solid lacrosse and soccer player, and a good friend to many. He is once again at home and in place.

On Mother's Day 2010, big sister Emma, Drew, Mitsuko, and I went to dinner at the Danfords Inn in Port Jefferson, right on the water, where the ferries come and go across Long Island Sound. At the end of a very windy but sunny and clear day, we sat upstairs, looking over the waves. One year earlier, when we were still settling into our new home, Mother's Day had been a mixed bag. Tensions were high and smiles were few. But now, thank heavens, we were happier and feeling whole again.

Emma, who had moved to Manhattan from Washington, D.C., just a few months before we came east, was happily talking about her guy friend, whom we met at Easter weekend and liked a lot. We laughed when we remembered how much we had struggled with this move, now a thing of the past. We talked about Mitsuko's trip back to Japan, planned for the summer, and about Lebron James and the Cleveland Cavaliers. Lebron did eventually move on, but he retains his Akron roots. Had he asked me, I would have told him to stick with Ohio.

Twenty-one months after our move, we were past all the peaks and valleys of 2008 and 2009, and we felt like more of a family than we ever had. Emma and Drew were closing the ten-year age gap between them and becoming close, although Drew did refer to Emma, at twenty-six, as "old" and a little out of touch. Again, we all laughed. You cannot love people if you cannot laugh with them. Mirth is a major virtue close to love, because in laughter everyone is having the same experience as one, and boundaries between selves evaporate.

And thank God we were laughing again, because mirth and rejoicing can help us survive in an uncertain world. In 2010, the State of New York is worse off economically than Greece. Threats of a government shutdown are real, and this state is not managed as well as Ohio. In May, as a member of the state university system, I was about to be "furloughed" one day a week until the dysfunctional legislators in Albany could get it together to pass a belated budget. That comes to 20 percent of my income, which is a lot when you have a mortgage. Our real estate guy says it will be 2012 at the earliest before the value of our property begins to recover. Taxes are crazy in New York State, and they will get crazier. And on May 6, 2010—my birthday—the stock market dropped a thousand points in a "flash crash" before rebounding. It continues to go up and down, along with my 401K, but I am not expecting any miracles.

I think that life in America is going to have to get a lot less materialistic and crass, and that we as a nation are going to have to rethink our views on happiness and how to live our lives meaningfully. Right now, our little family is coming together again, a little more mature, and more appreciative of one another than I can remember. And I know that we will be there for one another, come what will.

That Mother's Day evening, after we got home, I got a call from Julie Norman, my high school dorm mother who, after all these years, is still fulfilling that maternal role. It is good to have few people in life who remember you from early on. As she said, "Back then, you were different from most. I thought that you would either fail miserably or succeed wonderfully. You were definitely not heading for Wall Street. You stuck with your dreams, and you have done well." We left it that I would visit her in September.

And then I sat down in my office to start writing an article on oxytocin nasal spray. Oxytocin, the "compassion hormone," is being used experimentally in autistic children; and in "game theory" experiments, the spray causes subjects to make more generous and forgiving moves. I am wondering if oxytocin enhancement will become commonplace . . . I can think of a few occasions when I would welcome the opportunity to use it! For most of us, though, it will suffice to do "unto others"—the effects last a lifetime, not just a few hours.

Emma came in and said that the Celtics beat the Cavs. Oh well, maybe next year. Drew was chatting on the computer with his new girlfriend, and Mitsuko was doing the laundry. I said good night and went to bed. But before I turned the lights out, I read this prayer from the 8 A.M. service I had attended early that Sunday at All Soul's Episcopal Church in Stony Brook Village. It is from *The Book of Common Prayer*:

O God, who hast prepared for those who love thee such good things as pass man's understanding: Pour into our hearts such love toward thee, that we, loving thee in all things and above all things, may obtain thy promises, which exceed all that we can desire; through Jesus Christ our Lord, who liveth and reigneth with thee and the Holy Spirit, one God, for ever and ever. *Amen.*

A lot of good things are happening in our lives, some of which will exceed all that we can desire, and I have no doubt that there are good surprises ahead. Our journey together is not yet finished, but years hence we will probably retire back in Cleveland.

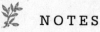

NOTES

Introduction: On the Move

1. For a set of twenty-eight scientific papers in general support of this idea, please see Stephen G. Post (ed.), *Altruism and Health: Perspectives from Empirical Science* (New York: Oxford University Press, 2007).

2. Alexis de Tocqueville, *Democracy in America* (New York: Penguin Books, 2003), p. 623. (Originally published 1835.)

3. These associations are solid, even when parental education, income, and race are controlled for. Personality moderates these findings. When you are forced to move from a place where you were deeply at home, it helps a lot to be an extrovert who easily rebuilds social networks and relationships. Extroverts can be blissfully unmoved by moves. But for more introverted personalities, for the moodier or high strung, the burdens are a lot greater. For a solid summary of existing research findings, see Shigehiro Oishi and Ulrich Schimmack, "Residential Mobility, Well-Being, and Mortality," in *Journal of Personality and Social Psychology*, 2010, 98(6), 980–994.

Chapter 1: Learning to Travel on Life's Mysterious Journey

1. See Edward S. Casey, *Getting Back into Place: Toward a Renewed Understanding of the Place-World*, 2nd ed. (Bloomington: Indiana University Press, 2009), p. xvi.

2. Robert D. Putnam, *Bowling Alone: The Collapse and Revival of American Community* (New York: Simon & Schuster, 2001).

3. Putnam, *Bowling Alone*, p. x.

4. See Stephen G. Post (ed.), *Altruism and Health: Perspectives from Empirical Science* (New York: Oxford University Press, 2007).

5. Esther Sternberg, *Healing Spaces: The Science of Place and Well-Being* (Cambridge, Mass.: Harvard University Press, 2009).

Chapter 2: The Gift of the "Giver's Glow"

1. David C. McClelland and Carol Kirchnit, "The Effect of Motivational Arousal Through Films on Salivary Immunoglobin A," *Psychology and Health*, 1988, 2(1), 31–52.

2. Charles Darwin, in *The Descent of Man and Selection in Relation to Sex* [London: Murray, 1871], p. 166, in his famous passage on the evolutionary origins of morality and benevolence, writes, "There can be no doubt that a tribe including many members who, from possessing in a high degree the spirit of patriotism, obedience, courage, and sympathy, were always ready to aid one another, and to sacrifice themselves for the common good, would be victorious over most other tribes; and this would be natural selection." Here Darwin is stating that helping others and contributing unselfishly to the well-being of the community is essential for the success and survival of the group. Thus, the fact that we have such remarkable human capacities for self-giving is evolution's greatest gift to us. It was never Darwin's view that evolution leads only, or even primarily, to selfishness. But how do we get rid of group conflicts?

3. "Selfish Genes Make Humans Selfless, New Theory Suggests," University of Michigan News Service, July 24, 2006, www.ns.umich.edu/?Releases/2006/Jul06/r072406a.

4. Jorge Moll and others, "Human Fronto-Mesolimbic Networks Guide Decisions About Charitable Donation," *Proceedings of the National Academy of Sciences*, 2006, *103*(42), 15623–15628.

5. The Do Good Live Well survey was released by United Healthcare and VolunteerMatch. For more information, please visit www.VolunteerMatch.org.

6. U.S. volunteering results for all fifty states and nearly two hundred cities can be found at VolunteeringinAmerica.gov, which hosts the most comprehensive set of statistics on volunteering available.

7. Joseph E. Kahne and S. Sporte, "Developing Citizenship," *American Educational Research Journal*, 2008, *45*(3), 738–766.

8. See www.universalgiving.org.

9. See Alina Tugend, "The Benefits of Volunteerism, If the Service Is Real," *New York Times*, July 31, 2010, p. B5.

10. Heather Johnston Nicholson, Christopher Collins, and Heidi Holmer, "Youth as People: The Protective Aspects of Youth Development in After-School Settings," *Annals of the American Academy of Political and Social Science*, 2004, *591*(1), 55–71.

11. Peter L. Benson, E. Gil Clary, and Peter C. Scales, "Altruism and Health: Is There a Link During Adolescence?" in Stephen G. Post (ed.), *Altruism and Health: Perspectives from Empirical Science* (New York: Oxford University Press, 2007).

12. See Micelle Dillon and Paul Wink, *In the Course of a Lifetime* (Berkeley: University of California Press, 2007). The authors examined nearly two hundred individuals who had participated for a lifetime in a study that was initiated in the 1920s at the University of California, Berkeley, through the Institute for Human Development. Youngsters ages ten to twelve were followed every ten years into the 1990s. Dillon and Wink asked, "Do generative qualities in adolescents predict better mental and

physical health in adulthood?" Generativity, defined as behavior indicative of positive emotions extending to all humanity, was measured in three dimensions: givingness, prosocial competence, and social perspective. The authors examined the longitudinal data and interviewed 180 of the original participants. They found that altruistic, helping attitudes in youth predicted mental and physical health across the lifespan. Despite limitations of the study noted by the authors themselves, the study lends crucial support to the notion that it is good to be good, and that the benefits of altruism accrue across a lifetime.

13. Frank Riessman, "The 'Helper' Therapy Principle," *Social Work*, 1965, *10*(2), 27–32.

14. G. A. Rogeness and R. A. Badner, "Teenage Helper: A Role in Community Mental Health," *American Journal of Psychiatry*, 1973, *130*, 933–936.

15. Maria E. Pagano, Karen B. Friend, J. Scott Tonigan, and Robert L. Stout, "Helping Other Alcoholics in Alcoholics Anonymous and Drinking Outcomes: Findings from Project MATCH," *Journal of Studies in Alcoholism*, 2005, *65*(6), 766–773.

16. Maria E. Pagano and others, "Helping Others and Long-Term Sobriety: Who Should I Help to Stay Sober? *Alcoholism Treatment Quarterly*, 2009, *27*(1), 38–50.

17. Maria E. Pagano, Sarah E. Zemore, Casey C. Ondor, and Robert L. Stout, "Predictors of Initial AA-Related Helping: Findings from Project MATCH," *Journal of Studies in Alcohol and Drugs*, 2009, *70*(1), 117–125.

18. New York State Office of Mental Health. "Self-Help and Peer Support," 2006, www.omh.state.ny.us/omhweb/News/Quality _Urban_Behavioral_Health/From_Vision_to_Practice.html.

19. Nancy Tomes, *The Art of Asylum-Keeping: Thomas Story Kirkbride and the Origins of American Psychiatry* (Philadelphia: University of Pennsylvania Press, 1984).

20. Personal interview with a representative of the International Center for Clubhouse Development. See also "Mission," www.iccd.org/mission.html.

21. Lori D'Angelo, interview, Apr. 6, 2007. For more information on Magnolia Clubhouse, please visit www.magnoliaclubhouse.org.

22. Stephanie L. Brown, Robert M. Brown, James S. House, and Dylan M. Smith, "Coping with Spousal Loss: The Potential Buffering Effects of Self-Reported Helping Behavior," *Personality and Social Psychology Bulletin*, 2008, 34, 849–861.

23. In a study that goes back to 1983, researchers at the University of California analyzed the speech patterns of 160 Type A personality subjects. The study showed that high numbers of self-references in speech significantly correlated with heart disease, after controlling for age, blood pressure, and cholesterol. The researchers suggested that a healthier heart can result when a person listens attentively when others talk, is more giving, and engages in unselfish acts. See Larry Scherwitz and others, "Type A Behavior, Self-Involvement, and Coronary Atherosclerosis," *Psychosomatic Medicine*, 1983, 45(1), 47–57.

24. Further research on hostility and coronary disease was conducted by Redford B. Williams, the distinguished cardiologist at Duke University. Williams used fifty questions pertaining to hostile emotions, attitudes, and actions from the Minnesota Multiphasic Personality Inventory (MMPI) to form the "hostility scale." Colleagues studied 255 doctors who had taken the inventory in the late 1950s while in medical school at the University of North

Carolina. As they aged from twenty-five to fifty, the doctors whose hostility scores were in the upper half were four to five times more likely than those with lower scores to develop coronary disease, and nearly seven times more likely to die of any disease. Similar results were found with many others groups, including employees of Western Electric, who showed increased cancer deaths as well. Among a group of law students at the University of North Carolina who took the MMPI in 1950, fully 20 percent with hostility scores in the highest quarter of their class had died by age fifty, in contrast with only 4 percent of those in the lowest quarter. Roughly the same outcome was found among medical students. See Redfield Williams and Virginia Williams, *Anger Kills: Seventeen Strategies for Controlling the Hostility That Can Harm Your Health* (New York: Harper Perennial, 1994).

25. A study at Ohio State University's Institute for Behavioral Medicine Research using the hostility scale with forty-two married couples showed that negative emotional states affect wound healing. Wounds took a day longer to heal after an argument than after supportive discussion, and two days longer in persons demonstrating high levels of hostility when compared to their low-hostility counterparts. See Janice K. Kiecolt-Glaser and others, "Hostile Marital Interactions, Proinflammatory Cytokine Production, and Wound Healing," *Archives of General Psychiatry*, 2005, *62*(12), 1377–1384.

   There are certain forms of cancer that research suggests have a relationship to emotional states. See Janice K. Kiecolt-Glaser and others, "Psycho-Oncology and Cancer: Psychoimmunology and Cancer," *Annals of Oncology*, 2002, *13*, 165–169.

26. Research on kindness and volunteerism in relation to health is thought to have begun in 1981 with a study that compared

volunteer workers and nonvolunteers over the age of sixty-five. K. I. Hunter and Margaret Lin found that the volunteers were significantly higher in life satisfaction and will to live, and they had fewer symptoms of depression and anxiety. Although Hunter and Lin could not formally determine a cause-and-effect relationship—raising the question of whether life satisfaction gave rise to volunteerism or vice versa—they indicated that the elderly volunteers themselves believed that their volunteer activities changed their lives for the better. See K. I. Hunter and Margaret W. Linn, "Psychosocial Differences Between Elderly Volunteers and Non-Volunteers," *International Journal of Aging and Human Development*, 1980–81, *12*(3), 205–213.

27. Phyllis Moen, Donna Dempster-McClain, and Robin M. Williams, "Social Integration and Longevity: An Event History Analysis of Women's Roles and Resilience," *American Sociological Review*, 1989, *54*(4), 635–647.

28. Alex H. Harris and Carl E. Thoreson, "Volunteering Is Associated with Delayed Mortality in Older People: Analysis of the Longitudinal Study of Aging," *Journal of Health Psychology*, 2005, *10*(6), 739–752. The authors concluded, "We found that more frequent volunteering is associated with delayed mortality even when the effects of socio-demographics, medical and disability characteristics, self-ratings of physical activity and social integration and support are controlled. The effect of volunteering on mortality appears to be more than a proxy for the well-known effects of social support, health, age, and other variables."

29. Marc A. Musick, A. Regula Herzog, and James S. House, "Volunteering and Mortality Among Older Adults: Findings from a National Sample," *Journal of Gerontology*, 1999, *54B*(3), S173–S180. See also Marc A. Musick and John Wilson,

"Volunteering and Depression: The Role of Psychological and Social Resources in Different Age Groups," *Social Science and Medicine*, 2003, *56*(2), 259–269; Mark A. Musick and John Wilson, *Volunteers: A Social Profile* (Bloomington: Indiana University Press, 2008).

30. Doug Oman, Carl E. Thoreson, and Kay McMahon, "Volunteerism and Mortality Among Community-Dwelling Elderly," *Journal of Health Psychology*, 1999, *4*(3), 301–316.

31. See Stephanie Brown, Randolph M. Nesse, Amiram D. Vonokur, and Dylan M. Smith, "Providing Social Support May Be More Influential Than Receiving It: Results from a Prospective Study of Mortality," *Psychological Science*, 2003, *14*(4), 320–327.

32. For more information about the Face of America Project, please visit www.faceofamericawps.com.

Chapter 3: The Gift of Connecting with the Neediest

1. Richard G. Tedeschi, Crystal L. Park, and Lawrence G. Calhoun (eds.), *Posttraumatic Growth: Positive Changes in the Aftermath of a Crisis* (New York: Routledge, 1998), p. 2.

2. S. J. Picot, S. M. Debanne, E. H. Namazi, and M. I. Wycle, "Religiosity and Perceived Rewards of Black and White Caregivers," *Gerontologist*, 1997, *37*(1), 89–101.

3. To learn more about the Sobriety Garden, please visit www.friends ofthesobrietygarden.org.

4. For more information, please visit www.helpingotherslivesober.org.

Chapter 4: The Gift of Deep Happiness

1. Prosperity is not doing us Americans all that much good when it comes to happiness. We are no happier today than we were in the early 1950s, despite huge increases in property and wealth,

bigger houses, more cars, and relentlessly escalating consumption. And there are many poorer countries where people report themselves as happier than do those in countries that are much more prosperous. See David G. Myers, *The American Paradox: Spiritual Hunger in an Age of Plenty* (New Haven, Conn.: Yale University Press, 2000).

2. Carol Nickerson, Norbert Schwarz, Ed Deiner, and Daniel Kahneman, "Zeroing in on the Dark Side of the American Dream: A Closer Look at the Negative Consequences of the Goal of Financial Success," *Psychological Science*, 2003, *14*(6), 531–536.

3. *Time*/SRBI, "The Science of Happiness" [poll], www.srbi.com/ time_happiness_12-15-455pm.pdf. The poll, conducted Dec. 13– 14, 2004, asked what people considered a major reason for their happiness. The top three sources of happiness were "relationship with children" (77 percent), "friends and friendships" (76 percent), and "contributing to the lives of others" (75 percent).

4. Pew Research Center, "Are We Happy Yet?" [poll], Feb. 13, 2006, http://pewresearch.org/pubs/301/are-we-happy-yet.

5. The National Study of Youth and Religion is the largest and most detailed study of teens and religion ever conducted. It included a nationwide telephone survey of teens and their parents, as well as in-depth face-to-face interviews with more than 250 of the respondents. The telephone survey of 3,290 English- and Spanish-speaking children between thirteen and seventeen, and their parents, was conducted between July 2002 and Apr. 2003. Christian Smith, author of *Soul Searching: The Religious and Spiritual Lives of American Teenagers* (New York: Oxford University Press, 2009) says, "The Devoted are more than twice as likely than the Disengaged to say they care very much about the needs of the poor and elderly people in the United States" (p. 229).

Religious teens "appear to possess greater moral compassion and concern for justice than their nonreligious peers—and apparently for religiously-related reasons and not simply because of differences in their domestic compositions" (p. 229).

6. The four aspects of happiness presented in this chapter are based on a detailed reading of existing research, my interactions with many positive psychologists, and my teaching and lecturing.

7. Joyce Millman, "Fred Rogers," Aug. 10, 1999, www.salon.com/people/bc/1999/08/10/rogers/index.html.

8. To learn more about L'Arche Farm and Gardens, please visit www.larchethc.org/C-FarmGardens/C1-FarmGardens.html.

9. Jean Vanier, *The Heart of L'Arche* (New York: Crossroad, 1995), p. 28.

10. Later published as "The Care of the Patient," *Journal of the American Medical Association*, 1927, 88, 877–882.

11. Joshua Wolf Shenk, *Lincoln's Melancholy: How Depression Challenged a President and Fueled His Greatness* (Boston: Houghton Mifflin, 2005), p. 189.

12. Some researchers estimate that about half of our happiness is due to how we are wired, but I think they are giving too much determining power to our genes. For example, see Sonja Lyubomirsky, *The How of Happiness: A New Approach to Getting the Life You Want* (New York: Penguin Books, 2007). In general, the power of the gene to determine behavior is overstated.

13. Whereas some researchers say that external circumstances only constitute about 10 percent of the happiness pie, I think that common ordinary experience and wisdom suggest that circumstances matter a bit more than this. See, for example, Anthony Kenny and Charles Kenny, *Life, Liberty and the Pursuit of Utility* (Exeter, England: Imprint Academic, 2006).

14. Lyubomirsky, *The How of Happiness.*

15. Cami Walker, *29 Gifts: How a Month of Giving Can Change Your Life* (Philadelphia: De Capo Lifelong Books, 2009).

Chapter 5: The Gift of Compassion and Unlimited Love

1. For more information on the Institute of Unlimited Love, please visit www.unlimitedloveinstitute.com.

2. See Tom W. Smith, "Spiritual and Religious Transformations in America: The National Spiritual Transformation Study," National Opinion Research Center/University of Chicago, Dec. 9, 2005, www-news.uchicago.edu/releases/05/121305 .norc.pdf.

3. For the survey instrument, see www3.uakron.edu/sociology/ flameweb/natsurvey/National_Survey_Questions.pdf.

4. Of the 21 percent of respondents in the "Never or not asked" and "Once in a while" categories, a little less than half were in the hard-core "Never or not asked" group. In detail, 17 percent experience God's love "most days"; 32 percent, "every day"; and 9.8 percent, "more than once a day." Another 10.8 percent feel this love "some days"; and 11.8 percent, "once in a while."

5. With regard to the frequency with which people experience God's love as increasing their compassion for others, the responses were as follows: "once in a while," 13.2 percent; "some days," 16.7 percent; "most days," 21.2 percent; "every day," 24.5 percent; "more than once a day," 7 percent.

6. Women and nonwhites were more likely to score higher on experiences of divine love than were white men. Other demographic indicators of this adult survey—age, education, income, and marital status—were not found to account for differences in divine love scores.

Chapter 6: The Gift of Hope

1. Hilary A. Tindle and others, "Optimism, Cynical Hostility, and Incident Coronary Heart Disease and Mortality in the Women's Health Initiative," *Circulation*, 2009, *120*, 656–662.

2. Shelley E. Taylor and Margaret E. Kemeny, "Psychological Resources, Positive Illusions and Health," *American Psychologist*, 2000, *55*(1), 99–109.

3. See Jerome Groopman, *The Anatomy of Hope: How People Prevail in the Face of Illness* (New York: Random House, 2005); chap. 7, "The Biology of Hope," is a terrific summary of what we know about how hope as an affective state affects the brain and the immune system. See also Esther Sternberg, *Healing Spaces: The Science of Place and Well-Being* (Cambridge, Mass.: Harvard University Press, 2009); chap. 8, "Hormones of Hope and Healing," is an outstanding presentation of the hard science around the ways in which hope affects physiological healing. An earlier study of value is Louis A. Gottschalk, Janny Fronczek, and Monte S. Buchsbaum, "The Cerebral Neurobiology of Hope and Hopelessness," *Psychiatry*, 1993, *56*(3), 270–281.

4. Sternberg, *Healing Spaces*. See also Edward S. Casey, *Getting Back into Place: Toward a Renewed Understanding of the Place-World* (2nd ed.) (Bloomington: Indiana University Press, 2009).

5. See Barbara Fredrickson, *Positivity: Groundbreaking Research Reveals How to Embrace the Hidden Strength of Positive Emotions, Overcome Negativity, and Thrive* (New York: Crown Archetype, 2009).

6. For more information about Brooke Ellison, please visit www .brookeellison.com.

7. Howard Thurman, *The Centering Moment* (Richmond, Ind.: Friends United Press, 2000), p. 29. (Originally published 1969.)

❧ ACKNOWLEDGMENTS

My work on this book was supported by the Center for the Study of Law and Religion at Emory University and by the John Templeton Foundation. It also was made possible with support from the Helping Others Live Sober Project (www.helpingotherslivesober.org) at Case Western Reserve University, and the Flame of Love Project (www.godlylove project.org) at the University of Akron.

In no way would I have written this particular book without sitting down for a luncheon conversation with Loretta Barrett and Sheryl Fullerton. Loretta is the kind of book agent who really does care about where a writer is heading long term, and she devoted a lot of her time to helping me think through big questions. Sheryl Fullerton, my editor at Jossey-Bass, encouraged the idea of a book at a personal story as a trajectory or, as she put it, an "arc." Had she not done so, this particular book would not have been written.

Naomi Lucks provided the great service of taking each chapter that I submitted to her and shaping it up into a clearer and more engaging presentation. We passed each chapter back and forth at least four or five times, and because our synergy was so good, the product is vastly better than it would otherwise have been. These three women together made all the difference. Few writers could be so fortunate.

I thank some of the really special people I have met at Stony Brook University, including Elisa Nelson; Brooke Ellison and her parents, Jean and Ed; Jack Coulehan; Maria Basile; Michael Vetrano; Richard Bronson; Lynn Hallarman; Iris Granek; Elizabeth Seaman; John Riley; Richard Fine; Eva Kittay; the Lymph Notes; and scores of others. Most of all, I thank the good people who traveled from California and Michigan, bearing in their own lives the challenges of big moves. Carla Keirns, Andrew Flescher, Stephanie Brown, and Dylan Smith are an outstanding group of colleagues, and I am daily honored to work with them. Carla's husband, Michael Dorn, and Stephanie and Dylan's children, Michael and Christopher, have to be thanked for coming along and for contributing as well. Michael Roess, a graduate assistant for the Center, has been great throughout it all.

Thanks to Clevelanders—to the hundreds of them who have kept in touch, who have stayed loyal, who have demonstrated the enduring qualities of the goodness that I believe defines very special people in a very special place. Thanks to the people of Case Western Reserve University, especially Bob Haynie and Kent Smith, and to Dick and Judy Watson, Cathy and John Lewis, Joni Marra, Matt Lee, Margaret Poloma, Maria Pagano, Pastor Otis Moss Jr., and Sara Miller.

Thanks to the John Fetzer Institute.

Most of all, I thank Mitsuko, Drew, and Emma for enduring this move and for sticking together as a family during a challenging time. They make me feel proud.

THE AUTHOR

Stephen G. Post, Ph.D. (University of Chicago), is founder and director of the Center for Medical Humanities, Compassionate Care, and Bioethics at Stony Brook University. Prior to his arrival at Stony Brook University, he was professor of medical ethics, philosophy, and religious studies in the School of Medicine at Case Western Reserve University. Post is widely known for his writings on caring for persons with dementia and for research at the interface of selfless love, science, and spirituality. He is an Elected Fellow of the College of Physicians of Philadelphia for "distinguished contributions to medicine"; he received the Kama Book Award in Medical Humanities from World Literacy Canada in 2008, and received the Distinguished Service Award from the National Alzheimer's Associated Board for "distinguished service to families." Post received the Hope in Healthcare Award in 2008 for his "pioneering research and education in the field of unconditional love, altruism, compassion, and service." Post is a public intellectual who has written for or been interviewed by such diverse periodicals as *Parade, O: The Oprah Magazine*, the *New York Times*, and *Psychology Today*. He is a lifelong member of the Episcopal Church and serves on the board of trustees of the John Templeton Foundation.

INDEX

A

Addiction, 69–70, 79–84

Agape love, 119–120, 123–124, 143–144, 165. *See also* Love; Unlimited Love

Alcoholics Anonymous, 36–38, 69

Alcoholism, and Sobriety Garden, 79–84

Altruism, 125–127

Alzheimer's disease, 58–63, 77–78

Amanda, story of, 163–164

Ambrosia, story of, 152–155

Amish community, 18–21

"Angelism," 132

Angola Prison, 153

Aristotle, 115

B

Barrett, E., 69–70

Barrett, L., 139

Basil of Caesarea, Saint, 136

Beauty, and hope, 159

Beck, C., 140

Behavior, and happiness, 112–113

Bellevue Hospital, and Sobriety Garden, 79–84

Benevolence, vs. violence, 130–131

Bereavement, 42

Bowling Alone: The Collapse and Revival of American Community (Putnam), 8–9

Brahmanism, 100

Brain, and helper therapy principle, 30–35

The Brooke Ellison Story (film), 161–164

Brown, M., 31

Brown, S., 30–31, 42

Buddhism, 99, 126

C

Campbell, J., 108

Care-connection system, 30–35

Case Western Reserve University School of Medicine, vii
Casey, E. S., 8
Cerebral palsy, 66–68
Children, and happiness, 92
Christianity, 99–100, 126
"Cognitive and Emotional Health Project—the Healthy Brain," 31
Cognitively impaired persons, 58–63, 78–79, 104–105
Coincidence, 134–140, 145–146
Compassion, 106–109, 140–145
"Confirmation bias," 138
Confucianism, 99
Connectedness, 132–134
1 Corinthians 13:13, 79
1 Corinthians 13:8, 169
2 Corinthians 9:7, 96, 169
Corporation for National and Community Service, 33
Cox, H., 128–129

D
D'Angelo, L., 39
Darwin, C., 29–30
Davis, G., 119–120, 123, 143
Deeply forgetful persons, 58–63, 78–79, 104–105
Dementia, 58–63, 78–79, 104–105

Depression, 38–39, 42–43, 110–111
The Descent of Man and Selection in Relation to Sex (Darwin), 29–30
Desire, and happiness, 90–91
Displacement, and stress, 9–10
Divine love scale, 128, 146–147
Dostoyevsky, F., 154–155
Drug addiction, 69–70, 79–84
Durkheim, E., 8

E
Egoism, 125–127
The Electric Kool-Aid Acid Test (Wolfe), 122
Ellison, B. M., 161–164
Embodied implacement, 8
Endorphins, 34
Environment, and happiness, 111–113
Ephesians 2:10, 168
Evolution, 29–30
Exodus, 21

F
Face of America Project, 47
Fetzer Institute, 137
Fillmore, C., 170
Fine, R. N., 167–168

Ford, H., 98
Forgiveness, 18–21, 140–145
Foundation House, 39
Frankl, V., 160
Fricchione, G., xiii
Friendships, 92, 114–115

G

Gardening, 149–150
Gates, B., 98
General Social Survey of the
    National Opinion Research
    Center, 127
Genetics, and happiness,
    111–113
"Giver's glow," definition of,
    12, 22
Giving behavior, and
    happiness, 92
God. *See* Unlimited Love
God-winks, 134–140, 145–146
Golden Rule, 99–100
Grace notes, 134–140, 145–146
Grafton Correctional
    Institute, 154
Granek, I., 12, 89
Granger-Brown, A., 155
Gratitude, 95, 103–106, 114
Green, J., 128
Gus, story of, 121–123

H

Happiness: and behavior,
    112–113; and environment,
    111–113; formula for, 94–95;
    and genetics, 111–113; and
    higher purpose, 95, 106–109;
    and income, 92–93; and
    love of others, 95–98; and
    marital status, 92–93; and
    moral integrity, 99–103; and
    spirituality, 93; and thankful
    simplicity, 95, 103–106, 114;
    types of, 90–94
Harris, A. H., 44
Healing, in place, 13–15
*Healing Spaces: The Science
    of Place and Well-Being*
    (Sternberg), 13
Health: and helper therapy
    principle, 28–29, 38–39; and
    hope, 151–152; and social
    integration, 8–9
Heart, and hope, 159–160
Helper therapy principle: benefits
    of, 27–30; and brain, 30–35;
    concept of, 35–38; and health,
    28–29, 38–39; and longevity,
    43–45; and mental illness,
    38–39, 40–43; and moving,
    21–22; and reaching out,

45–49; and religion, 51–53; and self-care, 49–51; and stress, 40–43; and volunteering, 32–35

"Helper's high," 33–35

"Helping-happiness loop," 113–115

Helping others. *See* Helper therapy principle

Helpingotherslivesober.org, 83

Higher purpose, and happiness, 95, 106–109

Hope: and beauty, 159; and Brooke Ellison, 161–164; and health, 151–152; and heart, 159–160; nature of, 152–157; and place, 157–161; and vision, 164–169

Hospitality, 9–10

Hwang, E., 71

I

Ilene, story of, 40–41

Immune system, 28–29

Income, and happiness, 92–93

Institute for Research on Unlimited Love, xii, 124, 165

Integrity. *See* Moral integrity

Intercessory prayer, 17

International Center for Clubhouse Development (ICCD), 39

Islam, 99

J

Jain, 100

James, W., 129

Janet S., story of, 69

Jim, story of, 57–58

Joyce, J., 22

K

Kahne, J. E., 34

Keller, H., 168

Kelly, C., 66–68

Kenny, S. S., 168

Kesey, K., 122

King, M. L., Jr., 120, 143

Kirkbride, T. S., 39

Knitting project, 64–66

Krishnamurti, J., 90–91

L

L'Arche Farm and Gardens, 104–105, 119

LaRue, J., 141

Laskey, S., 96

Lee, M., 128

Lincoln, A., 110, 112, 113, 160

Longevity, 43–45
Longitudinal Study of Aging, 44
Loretta Barrett Books, 139
Love: and cognitively impaired,
    78–79; and forgiveness, 20;
    nature of, 16–17; of others
    and happiness, 94–98; and
    scientific studies, 125–127;
    theology of, 120. *See also*
    Agape love; Unlimited Love
Loving kindness meditations, 17
Luke 14:12-14, 104
Luks, A., 33–34
Lymph Notes, 71–74
Lyubomirsky, S., 115–116

M
Magee, R., 81
Magnolia Clubhouse, 39
Marcus Aurelius, 105
Maritain, J., 132
Marital status, and happiness,
    92–93
Marshall, L., 101–103
Mastanduono, A., 71
Materialism, 90–92, 103–106
Mays, B. E., 77, 120, 143
McClelland, D., 28
Mead, A., 135–136
Melville, F., Jr., 84

Melville, W., 84
Mental illnesses, and helper
    therapy principle, 38–39,
    40–43
"Middle way," of Buddhism, 126
*The Moral Challenge of
    Alzheimer Disease* (Post), 60
Moral integrity, and happiness,
    94–95, 99–103
Moss, O., 142–144
Mother Teresa, 168
"Mother Teresa Effect," 28
Moving, and helper therapy
    principle, 21–22
Musick, M., 44

N
National Institute of Mental
    Health, 31
National Institute of
    Neurological Disorders and
    Stroke, 31
National Institute on Aging, 31
National Love and Forgiveness
    Campaign, 137
Nature, and hope, 157–161
Nelson, E., 12, 47–48,
    65–66, 167
New York University, and
    Sobriety Garden, 79–84

Nickel Mines, Pennsylvania, 18–21
Nix, O. R., 77
Norman, J., 174
Nouwen, H., 64

O

Oman, D., 44
Optimism, 152
"Order of love," in Christianity, 126
Oxytocin, 34, 174

P

Pagano, M. E., 37, 83
Pascal, B., 84
Paul, Saint, 168
Paul Simons Nature Preserve, 14, 22
Peabody, F. W., 107
Pew Research Center, 92–93
Place, role of, 13–15, 157–161
Polls, 91–93, 127–130
Poloma, M., 128
Post, G., 81
Post, M. M., 35
Post-traumatic growth (PTG), 74–78
Post-traumatic stress disorder (PTSD), 75

Posttraumatic Growth: Positive Changes in the Aftermath of a Crisis (Tedeschi, Park, and Calhoun, eds.), 75
Power, and happiness, 90
Prayer, 12, 17
Project MATCH, 37
Proverbs 29:18, 16, 165
Psalms 34:18, 76
Psalms 147:3, 76
Purpose in life, and happiness, 95, 106–109
Putnam, R. D., 8–9

Q

Quakers, 39

R

Reaching out, 45–49, 58–63
Reed College, 121–122
Reeve, C., 161
Relatedness, 132–134
Religion, and helper therapy principle, 51–53
Ricard, M., 19–20
Riessman, F., 36–37
Rogers, F., 100–101
Romans 8:28, 22
Romans 12:8, 169
Royce, J., 120

S

Sacred spaces, 13–15

Sadness, 109–111

Scattergood, T., 38–39

Schizophrenia, 38–39

Self-care, 49–51

Self-forgiveness, 20–21

Self-giving love, 125–127

Self-love, 125–127

Self, moving beyond, 63–74

Shanley, J., 98

Showalter, S., 137–138

Simplicity, 95, 103–106, 114

Slonaker, K., 71

Smith, D., 42

Smith, R., 36

Sobriety Garden, 79–84

Social connectedness, 92

Social integration, and health, 8–9

Sometimes a Great Notion (Kesey), 122

Spirituality: and happiness, 93; practice of, 15–17, 144–145, 170; and values, 165–166; in workplace, 12

Sternberg, E., 13, 157

Stony Brook University School of Medicine, vii, 3–5

Stress, 9–10, 40–43

Suicide (Durkheim), 8

Surveys, 91–93, 127–130

T

Taoism, 99

Templeton, J., 53, 113, 124, 127, 165–166

Thankful simplicity, and happiness, 95, 103–106, 114

Thoresen, C. E., 44

Thurman, H., 77, 120, 168

Tindle, H., 151

Tocqueville, A. de, x, xi

Trilling, J., 167

29 Gifts: How a Month of Giving Can Change Your Life (Walker), 115–116

Type A personality, 42–43

U

Underwood, L. G., 128–129

Unger, S., 166–167

Unlimited Love: and benevolence vs. violence, 130–131; and coincidence, 134–140; and compassion, 140–145; and forgiveness, 140–145; journey toward, 119–124; and relatedness, 132–134; and scientific studies, 125–127; survey on, 127–130. *See also Agape* love; Love

V

Vanier, J., 104–105, 119

The Varieties of Religious Experience (James), 129

Violence, vs. benevolence, 130–131

Vision, and hope, 164–169

Volunteering, 32–35

W

Walker, J. T., 121, 143

Wei, A., 72–73

Welles, R., 120, 140

Wilson, B., 36

Winfrey, O., 143

Wolfe, T., 122

Women's Health Initiative, 151

Workplace spirituality, 12

"Wounded healer," 64

Y

Yuen, F., 72

Z

Zoroastrianism, 99

Other Books of Interest

The Amish Way

Patient Faith in a Perilous World

Donald B. Kraybill, Steven M. Nolt, &
David L. Weaver-Zercher

Hardcover
ISBN: 978-0-470-52069-7

"*The Amish Way* is enlightening, practical, and well-researched. A wonderful read!"

> —**Beverly Lewis**, *New York Times* bestselling author of Amish fiction

"With detailed personal anecdotes and explanations straight from the Amish themselves, *The Amish Way* illustrates the simplicity and grace with which the Amish live their lives, and proves that those of us who have our own questions with faith might well learn from their example."

> —**Jodi Picoult**, author, *Plain Truth* and *House Rules*

In this follow-up to the bestselling *Amish Grace: How Forgiveness Transcended Tragedy*, the authors explore the complicated question, "Is there anything the Amish can teach the rest of us about living meaningfully in the modern world?"

DONALD B. KRAYBILL, Ph.D., is senior fellow at the Young Center of Elizabethtown College in Elizabethtown, Pennsylvania.

STEVEN M. NOLT, Ph.D., is professor of history at Goshen College in Goshen, Indiana.

DAVID L. WEAVER-ZERCHER, Ph.D., is professor of American religious history at Messiah College in Grantham, Pennsylvania.

Other Books of Interest

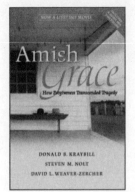

Amish Grace

How Forgiveness Transcended Tragedy

Donald B. Kraybill, Steven M. Nolt, &
David L. Weaver-Zercher

Paperback
ISBN: 978-0-470-34404–0

"A story our polarized country needs to hear: It is still grace that saves."
—**Bill Moyers,** Public Affairs Television

"In a world where repaying evil with evil is almost second nature, the Amish remind us there's a better way. In plain and beautiful prose, *Amish Grace* recounts the Amish witness and connects it to the heart of their spirituality."
—**Sister Helen Prejean**, author, *Dead Man Walking*

"A superb book—a model of clear, forceful writing about a tragedy and its aftermath. The authors have an obvious affection for the Amish yet ask tough questions, weigh contradictions, and explore conundrums such as how a loving God could permit schoolgirls to be massacred."
—**National Catholic Reporter**

Amish Grace tells the incredible story of the remarkable response of the Amish community to the horrific shooting of ten schoolgirls at Nickel Mines, PA, in October 2006. Now in paperback, this extraordinary, award-winning account of Amish forgiveness includes an afterword by the authors along with an interview with the mother of the man responsible for the shootings, and a guide for discussion.

Other Books of Interest

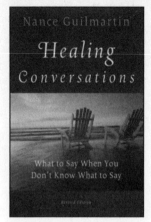

Healing Conversations

What to Say When You Don't Know What to Say

by Nance Guilmartin

> **978-0-470-60355-0**
> **Paperback | 240pp**

"Through real-life stories … Ms. Guilmartin shows how to be a helpful and comforting resource, how to listen as well as to talk, and, conversely, how to seek comfort in rough times."
—The *New York Times*

"I urge you to buy a copy of Healing Conversations . . . you'll feel more confident about your ability to know what to say and how to say it."
—Christiane Northrup, MD, renowned physician and author of *Women's Bodies, Women's Wisdom*

Healing Conversations helps gently guide communication when we can't seem to find the words. Using a collection of evocative stories about crucial situations, *Healing Conversations* is a timeless gift and an inspiring, definitive guide for reaching out to those who need support, comfort, and help.

Nance Guilmartin is a four-time regional Emmy Award–winning broadcast journalist, speaker, business advisor, executive coach, and community service advocate. Today she challenges organizations and executives to achieve breakthroughs and unlock hidden opportunities.